MAKEUP*for*
THEATRE, FILM,
& TELEVISION

MAKEUP *for* THEATRE, FILM, & TELEVISION

A Step by Step Photographic Guide

by

LEE BAYGAN

A & C BLACK · LONDON
DRAMA BOOK PUBLISHERS · NEW YORK

First published in Great Britain 1984
Reprinted 1987
A & C Black (Publishers) Limited
35 Bedford Row, London WC1R 4JH

Originally published by Drama Book Publishers,
260 Fifth Avenue, New York, New York 10001, USA

© Copyright 1982 by Lee Baygan

Reprinted for both imprints in 1989, 1991, 1994 by
A & C Black (Publishers) Limited.

ISBN 0-7136-2430-2 (UK)
ISBN 0-89676-093-6 (US)

**British Library Cataloguing in
Publication Data**

Baygan, Lee
   Makeup for theatre, film & television.
   1. Make-up, Theatrical   2. Film make-up
I. Title
790.2   PN2068

   ISBN 0-7136-2430-2

**Library of Congress Cataloging in
Publication Data**

Baygan, Lee
   Makeup for theatre, film & television.
   1. Make-up, Theatrical. I. Title.
PN2068.B39   792′.027   81-1911   AACR2

ISBN 0-89676-093-6

Printed in Great Britain by
BAS Printers Limited, Over Wallop, Stockbridge,
Hampshire

TO
CHARLI AND YOU

ACKNOWLEDGMENTS

In creating this book, I am most grateful to Barbara Armstrong, Barbara Kelly, Candace Carell, Marilyn Peoples, Werner Sherer, Anthony Cortino, Alan D'Angerio, Edward Jackson, Peter Wise, and John Caglione for allowing me to use their faces. I also want to thank those who have loaned me an ear, a nose, an eye, a chin, and a hand—figuratively as well as literally. I especially want to thank Patricia MacKay for her interest and encouragement and Bob Kelly for his concern, kindness, and support all along the line. Finally, there is Charli. I can't thank her enough for her helpful suggestions, contributions, and assistance.

CONTENTS

INTRODUCTION

We sat in the theatre—fifth row, center aisle—waiting for the curtain to rise. In my expectant mood I had quite forgotten the hot day waiting in line to get these good seats. Finally the house lights dimmed and the last whispers died down as the curtain went up on a beautiful set. Then, one by one, the characters made their entrances. I believe they were talking to one another, but I couldn't hear what they were saying. My attention was drawn, unavoidably, to the makeup.

There is an old saying that, when you pass his shop, the shoemaker looks at your shoes and the barber at your hair. It is not surprising then that I was stunned by the exaggerated, old-fashioned makeup. I was disappointed and irritated to have my mind taken away from the play in this way and, of course, dismayed that this approach to makeup still exists in the theatre. By the time I'd become used to the parade of "overstated" faces—and overcome memories of other times I'd been thus jolted (and jilted)—I'd lost much of the play, which is really why we were in the theatre in the first place. Every part of a theatrical production—costumes, sets, and lighting—is vitally important and no one thing should stand out from the working whole. Makeup is no exception.

Perhaps the idea of writing a book on makeup began to germinate that night. I remembered all those other nights I'd been made much too aware of the makeup—in Broadway and Off-Broadway productions, in regional theatres, and in community theatres and universities. I'm not saying that theatrical makeup is always heavy and overdone, but that all too frequently it is.

Old-fashioned theatrical makeup at its best is offensive to those in the front half of the orchestra section. Now someone might ask, "What about the people sitting from mid-orchestra to the last row, or those in the mezzanine and balconies? Surely the heaviness of the makeup won't bother them. In fact, it's probably very necessary." Apart from the fact that those people in the front orchestra seats are paying good money (these days, very good money) and deserve some consideration, it's important to remember that the farther back one sits, the smaller the faces appear. And, as this happens, thick lines and shadings appear closer together; they become compressed, and—depending upon the heaviness of the application—result in unrecognizable, even distorted faces. Furthermore, about mid-orchestra some people bring out their opera glasses. What do they see? The same thing as the people up front—heavily painted faces. At this point you'll probably ask another question. "Shouldn't the actors wear more makeup to compensate for the size of the theatre?" The answer is an emphatic no. Applying heavy theatrical makeup is an outmoded technique used not for the benefit of those sitting in the balcony but to compensate for inadequate lighting facilities. I'll be writing more about this later.

In the past seven years that I've been lecturing and demonstrating to theatre groups around the country, I've found that makeup is often viewed as the bastard child of the theatre, and that there are still producers and directors who do not consider makeup either an art or an important part of an actor's tools in creating a character. I've also found there are still performers who must regularly do their own makeup and who, if they're not trained in this technique, frequently find themselves relying on anyone around who can offer a helping hand. More often than not, however, the helper's ideas and approaches are outmoded; he simply cannot give an actor the professional guidance needed. Even when a makeup artist is present, as in film and TV, there are times an actor must know how to do his or her own makeup.

Thus this guidebook for those actors and actresses in theatre, opera, film, and television who might be interested in some of my ideas and techniques. To make the information as workable as possible, each chapter is complete in itself, repeating steps explained in previous chapters. If a certain type of makeup is desired, simply turn to that specific chapter and find the list of materials needed plus a step by step explanation in words and pictures. In the chapters noted "for black and for white performers," the technique and steps taken are the same for both skin colors. There is a difference, however, in the shades of foundation used, and in the corresponding highlights and shadows.

CHOICE OF FOUNDATION

Nowhere will there be any mention of a particular number or shade of foundation that must be used, for I believe it is the character being portrayed—not the actor, director, makeup artist, or anyone else—who will dictate the right shade of foundation.

As an actor, your makeup creation as well as your character creation begins when you get the script, not the night of dress rehearsal. After you've read it over a few times, you will have begun to create a mental picture of the character you'll be portraying. During the course of rehearsals you will learn many things about your character—his background, his lifestyle, the place and period in which he lives, his physical and mental health, his age, temperament, financial standing, social milieu, and other facts that will give insight into his character and appearance. It would be a good idea if you went to the library and

"boned up" on facial anatomy as well, during your period of study and research. A book on physiognomy would be an additional help.

By ferreting out all these facts, and working daily on your findings, you will build a true image of a character who is no longer you, no matter how closely you think you resemble him physically. You might call this work "inner makeup"—a preparation for the outer makeup that is to follow. This inner character will dictate your choice of makeup base, as well as your choice of color and the amount of rouge, lipstick, and eye shadow—in fact, the whole style of your makeup and much more. Working this way, it will be creative, not stereotyped, makeup.

Recall that familiar stereotype of the aged—the doddering old man with the squeaky, tremulous voice; the bald, shaking head; the sallow, painted face—all too often carried to the point of caricature. Let us remember, too, that not all young leading men are healthy and hirsute, nor all leading ladies fair-skinned and rosy-cheeked; neither do all Orientals have yellow skin.

No matter what the outcome of your character study, keep in mind that you are still using your own face with its own unique muscle and bone structure. Because of this individuality, which we all possess, I have divided this book into two parts.

Part One has no set rules. Not knowing your face, skin tone, or the character you are portraying, I cannot say what shade of foundation you should use or what approach you should take. The materials used and the steps taken in these chapters have been chosen specifically for the models I have selected and the characters I've had in mind. Although you can follow them if you're portraying similar characters, you won't get the same results because of the differences between your muscle and bone structure and those of my models. Part One is a guide to follow after you have discovered your character's "inner makeup"; you can eliminate steps not needed or add other steps from other chapters.

Part Two does have rules. If, for example, you want to create a scar, wear a bald cap, or lay on a beard, you must have certain specific items and take certain specific steps to achieve the desired result. This, of course, has nothing to do with your individual muscle and bone structure; it works the same for everyone.

STAGE MAKEUP AND THE SIZE OF THE THEATRE

The question "Aren't actors supposed to wear more makeup to compensate for the size of the theatre?" has already been answered in the negative at the beginning of this introduction. But I must state again—because of its importance—that actors who overcompensate with copious makeup have done so because of a theatre's inadequate lighting facilities and not because of its size. Today, with the adequate lighting available in all theatres and the general intimacy existing between actors and audience, we must rid ourselves of these overly-painted faces and move on to a more natural look. Of course, if you are in a deliberately dimly-lit production, you must apply more makeup to compensate for this design element.

When you have finished your makeup, be it straight or character, bearded or bald, look in your makeup mirror—which should be about five feet away from you, provided that the makeup room is furnished with sufficient lighting—and see how you look. If you do not look made-up, if you cannot detect the work and the materials used, your makeup will register in any theatre, regardless of its size. If you achieve this natural look in all

your makeups—and you will find this requires a lot of practice—this same makeup can be used for film and television where the natural look is preferred, because camera close-ups, color, and lighting have to be considered.

LIGHTING AND COLOR IN TELEVISION AND FILM

Each medium has its own technical problems, and makeup artists in both television and film know how to make the necessary adjustments; however, I believe that as a performer you should be aware of certain problems involved. Television lighting, in most dramatic shows using multi cameras, is overhead lighting, which creates unwanted shadows and can also make a mountain out of that little mole on your face. You are at the mercy of the lighting designer (known as the LD), and he has his hands tied because of the nature of television studios and the equipment involved. Here we are dealing with electronic shading, or "painting" as it is now called. With the equipment available at this time, isolation of some colors is not possible—that is, you cannot have a sharp separation between certain colors placed side by side; color "bleeding" is an almost constant headache for everybody involved. If, for instance, you are wearing green eyeshadow, the presence of a green chair, a green curtain, or a green dress on someone next to you will make the area around your eyes pick up a lot of green. If you have yellow pigment in your skin or hair coloring, a yellow or green tie or shirt can turn your face and hair yellowish. In such cases it is the costume designer's and set designer's task to watch out for color conflicts.

In film you won't have these complications, as colors do not present a problem and the lighting, which is placed at eye level, is in your favor.

LIGHTING AND COLOR IN THE THEATRE

If you look at the rainbow, you will find the sun spectrum, which consists of seven colors: red, orange, yellow, green, blue, indigo, and violet.

There are three primary colors: red, yellow, and blue. Mix them and you will form the secondary colors:

red + yellow = orange
yellow + blue = green
blue + red = violet

All colors are divided into three groups: warm, cool, and neutral. Warm colors are red, orange, yellow, and all their combinations. Cool colors are blue, indigo, and violet, and all their combinations. Black and white are considered neutral colors.

On stage, under amber and straw lights:
Rouge, depending on its tone, turns to orange or fades away completely.
Brown takes on a darker tone.
Blue turns to green.
Deep green changes to light brown.
Blue gray turns to deep slate.
Natural foundation appears pasty.

Under red lights:
Rouge and lipstick fade.
Blue and blue gray turn to violet.
Light brown disappears completely.
Deep green turns to a yellowish tone.
Brown becomes a very dark shade of brown.
Natural foundation becomes pale orange.

Under blue lights:
Pale rouge turns to dark violet.
Dark rouge turns into black violet, and at times, depending on its tone, it can even turn to dirty spots on the cheeks.
Lipstick turns to black.
Natural foundations generally turn to purple.

Under green lights:
Red turns to brown.
Brown becomes black.
Light and dark foundations become greenish.

There are other color gels and their combinations, and each one of them has some effect on your makeup.

Should you worry about the effect of color gels on your makeup? Should you change your makeup to compensate? When certain gels wash out your rouge and lipstick, yes, you can add more rouge and change your lipstick—just make sure you don't look overdone in the next scene. When there is a choice between effective lighting and the actor's face, however, the actor's face is more important. Anyone can accept red and green faces in a fantasy, a dream sequence, or a musical number. But how about a love scene in a serious play? Would you like to see two lovers looking magenta or blue in the moonlight?

HIGHLIGHT AND SHADOW

We see all objects three-dimensionally because of light, shade, highlight, and shadow. The best way to observe the play of lights on your face and create these highlights and shadows is to place a spotlight in front of you. Looking in your mirror—with the spotlight in front, placed so that the light is not blinding—you will not find much detail in your face. Move the light under your chin and you will see your muscle and bone structures in an unnatural form. Now hold the light on top of your head and you will see your face more or less as we see it during the day at noon. If you examine your face carefully from all angles you will see each section—depending on how your muscle and bone structures are constructed—as round or flat, with hard or soft edges forming wrinkles, nasolabial folds, apple cheeks, crow's feet, and frown lines. It is very important that you note what happens to your face as the light keeps moving around. In the makeup room you are stationary and the light is being moved around; on stage, or in film and television, you are moving around and the lights are stationary. To help yourself and the lighting director, you must be aware of your key lights at all times. So keep your head up and let them light your face fully.

While you are still in front of your makeup mirror, go over your entire face with your fingers, feeling every plane and projection, probing every nook and cranny so you come to understand its topography. Now make faces at yourself—cry, laugh, get angry— but always find a motivation for your crying, laughing, or raging, and in doing this you will see that your facial muscles will respond truthfully.

Color photographs have not been included in this book because I have seen too many actors blindly trying to copy the makeup colors they see in photographs—with the most unfortunate results. As you have probably realized by now, I do not prescribe any particular number or shade of makeup. I do not believe in rules or formulas except where, by necessity, they have to be followed, as in Part Two of this book. Rules only tie you down and stifle your creativity and imagination.

Do not give up if you cannot apply a certain technique or obtain a certain material. I have, wherever possible, provided alternatives; you can use your imagination and substitute alternatives of your own, try new materials, and improvise. Regarding improvising, you can even avail yourself of items from the kitchen cabinet, the dining table, and the wastepaper basket. In your search for excellence, you will come across other techniques and other materials. By all means try them and find the way that is best suited to your needs.

When you step on stage, for those of us sitting there watching, it matters little how you have prepared yourself, how long it has taken you, what problems you have had, what approaches you have taken, or what technique or materials you have used. Only the finished product counts. If it pleases us and we accept you as the character— without being aware of your makeup, hair style, costume, or acting technique—then you have succeeded. If not, there isn't much you can do except return to the drawing board. So let's return to the makeup table and begin at the beginning.

MAKEUP *for* THEATRE, FILM, & TELEVISION

PART ONE

1

Corrective Makeup

Corrective makeup means you are adding to or correcting what nature has given you—or taking away what you'd rather she hadn't. If you can use these pluses or minuses for your various characters, by all means do so. If you must correct them, this is how to go about it.

HAIR AND HAIRLINES

1–4.

To get rid of unwanted gray hair at the temple area and in the sideburns, or all over your head, try brown or black Roux hair coloring stick, using a toothbrush or eyebrow brush as an applicator. Make sure you are not also touching up your skin. Let dry and comb. It washes out with soap and water.

5–8.

If you have a receding hairline on top or at the temples, take a very sharp eyebrow pencil and carefully draw individual lines alongside the thin hairs you have. This makes the hair appear thicker. Do not smear the lines and do not use a greasy pencil that will shine and smear.

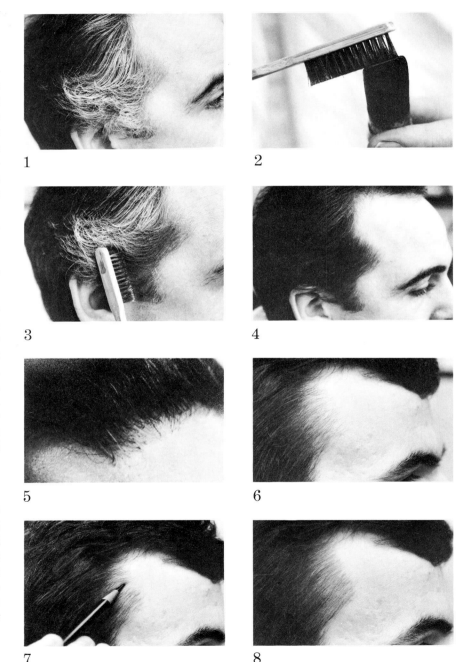

1

2

3

4

5

6

7

8

EYEBROWS

9–11.

If you have light eyebrows, light touches of eyebrow pencil on the hairs—not on your skin—will make the brows darker and fuller.

12–14.

If you have thin eyebrows or have plucked them to almost nothing, use a very sharp, soft lead pencil and feather strokes to create fine new brows that fit your character. Do not simply draw a hard line from one corner to the other and call it an eyebrow.

9

10

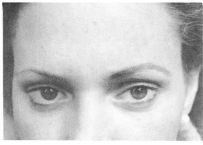

11

12

13

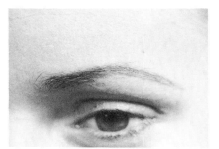

14

EYES

15–17.

If you have puffy eyelids, applying light shades of eyeshadows only makes them appear puffier. As a result, your eyes appear smaller. It is better to use dark shades of eyeshadow to make the puffiness less noticeable.

18–19.

If you have small eyes, it is advisable to line the top and bottom lids—perhaps with a smudgy line. Take care not to make your eyes look made-up and framed in harsh black lines. You can apply mascara if your eyelashes are blond or very thin.

15

16

17

18

19

20–22.

For women, apply an eyeshadow suitable for the character, as well as eyeliner on the top and a touch of shading at the bottom.

23.

Use artificial lashes of different length and thickness.

24–25.

Add highlights at the inner and outer corners of the eye to make the eyes seem wide open.

20

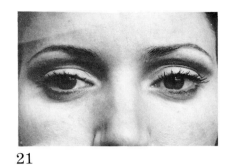

21

22

23

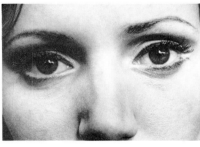

24

25

UNDER THE EYES

26–28.

If you have discoloration or circles under the eyes, a touch of highlight (usually a few shades lighter than the base) should help—providing the circles are not too dark. If the tone becomes grayish, omit the highlight and extend the foundation all the way up to the lower lashes; a touch of red to the foundation (such as Sunburn by Bob Kelly) is an additional help.

29.

If you have real pouches or bags under the eyes, getting rid of them is almost impossible. In film, lighting can often correct this situation and conceal other unwanted wrinkles and crevices as well.

26

27

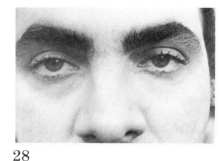

28

29

WIDE NOSE

30–32.

If you have a fairly wide nose or a slightly crooked one, you can thin or correct it by applying shading colors (usually a few shades darker than the foundation) on either side of the nose or on the side that needs to be straightened. Additional highlight should not be added in the center (the shading creates a thinning effect naturally), but a little might be necessary in the right place to correct a crooked nose.

30

31

32

LIPS

33–35.

If your lips are full but very colorless, a touch of Male Lip Color (Bob Kelly) or the shade closest to your lip color will do the job. Do not use regular women's lipstick shades.

36–38.

On the other hand, women with thin lips can outline the new lip line with a lip pencil of color appropriate to the character. Then, using the proper shade, fill in the rest. This is done only for stage, not for film or television.

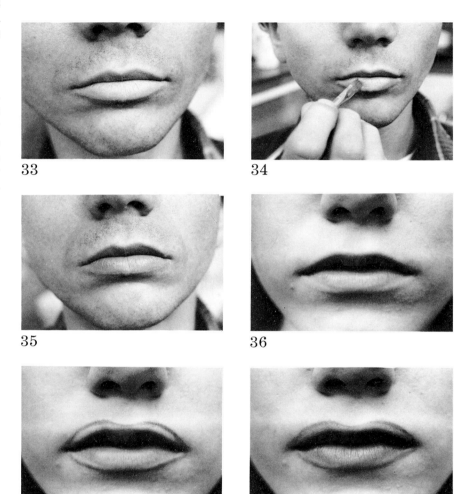

33

34

35

36

37

38

39–43.

If you have full lips and want to make them appear narrow and thin, first apply a coat of foundation and then outline the new lip size desired. Use lipstick appropriate for the character to achieve the desired result. This is done only for stage, not for film or television.

39

40

41

42

43

CHIN

44–45.

If you have a receding chin, a touch of highlight—blended at the edges into the foundation—can give a more pronounced impression. And, if a jutting chin is absolutely necessary, use a wax or latex piece (see Chapter 22, Nose and Chin). For men, depending on the age of the character and the appropriateness, a chin beard can also correct a receding chin.

44

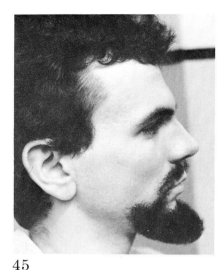

45

JAWLINE

46–48.

Should you shade your jawline if it is wider than the upper part of your face? You can if you want to, but only for the stage. This shading will not take anything away; your jaw will still be there, only darker. Another aid is a change of hairdo which creates a balance between the lower and upper part of the face.

46

47

48

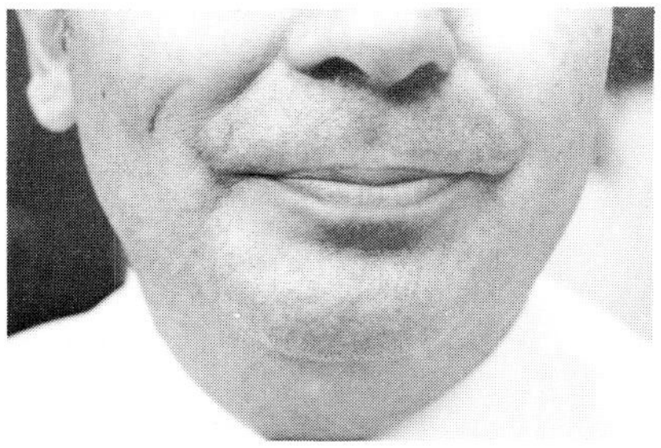

49

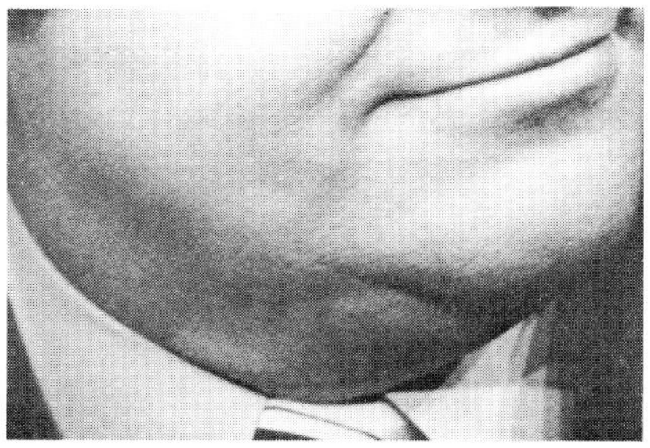

50

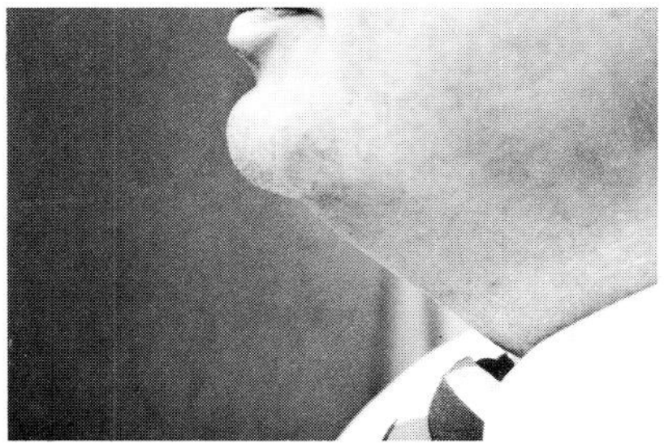

51

52

DOUBLE CHIN

49–52.

If you have what is known as double chin you can shade it darker if you want, but remember that the actual hanging muscle is still there—especially when you stand in profile and when you bend your head. On stage you might be able to create the illusion that your jawline is narrower and that your double chin is not there, but for television and film this kind of shading only creates a dirty, muddy area. Accept what you have and do the best you can using your own facial features to create the character.

All the corrective ideas suggested here can be used for film and television, except where otherwise indicated. Each one requires extreme care to achieve a completely natural look.

2

Straight Makeup for White Women

1

MATERIALS

1. Foundation (one shade or a combination of several shades)
2. Foam rubber sponge
3. Highlight (a few shades lighter than the foundation)
4. Shading (a few shades darker than the foundation), if necessary
5. Assorted brushes (eyebrow, eyeliner, powder, rouge, lipstick, and two ⅜" brushes for highlight and shading)
6. Cream and/or cake rouge
7. Eyeshadow
8. Translucent powder and puff
9. Eyebrow pencil
10. Cake eyeliner
11. Mascara
12. Artificial lashes
13. Scissors or a razor
14. Duo surgical adhesive
15. Toothpick or orange stick
16. Tweezers
17. Lipstick, lip gloss, or lip lining pencil

For information on choosing the right foundation, the corresponding highlight and shadow, and, in fact, the whole style of makeup for the character you are portraying, read "Choice of Foundation" on page xii of the Introduction.

APPLICATION

1.
Begin with a clean face.

2.
Apply foundation evenly and smoothly all over the face and neck with a foam rubber sponge. If you are mixing a few colors to get the right shade and tone for the character, hold them all in one hand. Wipe each one with the sponge to mix the colors, then apply.

2

3.
Highlight is used to cover dark circles or discoloration under the eyes. Sometimes, however, highlight will simply turn the discoloration grayish. If this happens, eliminate the highlight and use foundation instead, extending it all the way up to your eyelashes. A touch of red mixed with the foundation, such as Sunburn by Bob Kelly, can also be applied under the eyes to avoid this unwanted gray.

3

4

4.

If you have real bags under your eyes, however, there is little chance of completely concealing them with any amount of paint.

5.

Highlight can also be used in the deep crevices around the mouth, forehead, and nose.

6–7.

If you will be wearing cream rouge apply it now, before powdering your face. Using a foam rubber sponge as an applicator, place your rouge directly under the cheekbone and continue it up lightly over your bone structure to create three-dimensional features. (However, if you will be wearing cake rouge, you must apply it after you have powdered your face—see step 26–27.) If you have a very round face, stay away from this technique and apply cream or cake rouge where the normal cheek color is located.

8.

Choose an eyeshadow appropriate for the character you'll be portraying. The choice in this example is an off-white shade, which is applied over the lower part of the eyelid next to the lashes and all the way up to the crease.

9.

To create a three-dimensional eye a dark shade of eyeshadow is used between the end of the off-white shadings and the bone structure directly under the eyebrow. If you have very deep set eyes or very puffy eyelids, this technique will not work.

5

6

7

8

9

10.

Powder the entire face with translucent powder. *Do not rub.* Gently pat your face.

11.

Brush off excess powder.

12.

Use a sharp eyebrow pencil, as close to your own color as you can get, and fill in the thin areas of your brows. Darken only the light hairs. Do not draw a thick dark line from one side to another and call it an eyebrow. Use a feather stroke technique and brush to get an even shape.

13.

Eyeliner should be applied with an eyeliner brush. Use dark brown or black cake eyeliner. Don't use an eyebrow pencil because it will smear, and don't use liquid eyeliner because it will flake.

14.

Apply the mascara of your choice to the upper and lower lashes. If it gets on your skin, clean it off with a damp brush or Q-Tips. Don't use tissues or your fingers.

10

11

12

13

14

15

16

17

18

19

20

15.

If you are using artificial lashes they must be cut to size, unless yours do not need shaping. If they are too long lengthwise, cut a small section off and shape the rest. Usually the outer end of the strip is longer than the inner.

16.

You can thin and shape the lash strip by holding it in one hand and approaching the hairs at right angles with the tip of the scissors, snipping out unwanted hairs. Make some shorter than others.

17.

Another way of shaping is to place the lashes on a table and, holding the strip side and using a single-edge razor at right angles to the seam, snip out one hair at a time.

18.

Apply a small amount of Duo surgical adhesive to the bonded lash strip.

19.

Place the strip directly at the root of your lashes touching the skin. Never place it on top of your own lashes or your eyelids.

20.

Press the strip of lashes down with a toothpick, orange stick, or the end of a brush. Whichever you use, be careful. (A word of advice: whenever you're working on someone else's eyes, make sure the person's head is resting against the back of a chair.)

21.

If you prefer using individual lashes, take a pair of regular lashes and cut through the bonded edge, a few hairs at a time, with scissors or a single-edge razor.

22.

Place a drop of Duo surgical adhesive on a clean surface.

23–24.

Lift each section of hair with a tweezers and dip the end into the adhesive. Gently place the hairs next to your own lashes. Placement and amount depend on how thin or sparse your own lashes are. This can be done either before or after you have applied your mascara. The choice is yours, but make sure you do not lift and lose the hairs when applying mascara.

25.

A touch of dark brown pencil under the eyes would be nice. *Do not* draw a heavy black line. It should look like shading or smudge.

26–27.

Now, with your rouge brush, apply a touch of dry rouge where you applied cream rouge before—a touch over the chin, on the forehead, and maybe under the eyebrows at the outer end. All this will give you a pretty, alive, and natural look. Don't overdo it. Remember, you can always add more.

21

22

23

24

25

26

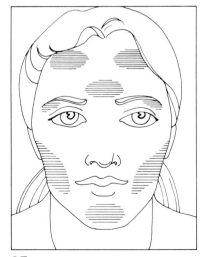

27

28

28.

Choose the right shade of lipstick. Stay away from heavy lip gloss—it will make your lips disappear. On the other hand, if you have naturally colored lips a touch of lip gloss might be sufficient for the character you are portraying. You can also outline your lips if you want—using a lip lining pencil—but don't overdo it. Make sure your hands, neck, and arms are made up before leaving the makeup room.

29.

Now you are ready.

If you choose the correct shade of foundation to match your skin tone, applying it lightly and following the steps explained here, you can appear in front of film and television cameras without any problems. Just remember that for television you should stay away from colored eyeshadows (use brown and off-white) and select a lipstick that has no blue in its formula.

29

Straight Makeup for Black Women

MATERIALS

1. Foundation (one or a combination of several shades)
2. Foam rubber sponge
3. Highlight (usually a few shades lighter than the foundation)
4. Shading (usually a few shades darker than the foundation), if necessary
5. Assorted brushes (eyebrow, eyeliner, powder, lipstick, rouge, and two ⅜" brushes for highlight and shading)
6. Cream and/or cake rouge
7. Eyeshadow
8. Translucent powder and puff
9. Eyebrow pencil
10. Dark brown or black cake eyeliner
11. Lipstick or lip gloss
12. Mascara
13. Artificial eyelashes (if needed)
14. Duo surgical adhesive
15. Toothpick or orange stick
16. Scissors or a single-edge razor blade
17. Tweezers

For information on choosing the right foundation, the corresponding highlight and shadow, and, in fact, the whole style of makeup for the character you are portraying, read "Choice of Foundation" on page xii of the Introduction.

APPLICATION

1.

Begin with a clean face. By now you probably have a good idea about your own skin tone (how dark it is, whether it is even in color, etc.) and that of your character.

2.

Using a foam rubber sponge, apply one or a combination of foundation colors over the face and neck, making sure the coverage is light and even. (If you are mixing colors, keep them all in one hand, rub the sponge over them, and then apply.)

3.

Using a foundation lighter than your skin tone will often give you a pasty look, but if your character is lighter skinned than you are, a careful choice of color can give the right effect.

1

2

3

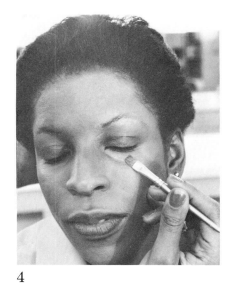

4

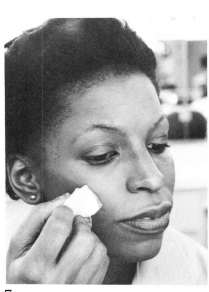

7

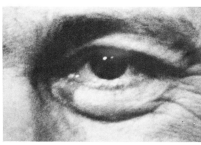

5

6

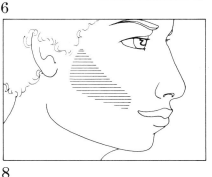

8

9

4.

Highlight is used to cover dark circles or discoloration under the eyes and under the nasolabial folds. If, in correcting this discoloration, your highlight shade does not look right (if there's too much of a contrast), eliminate the highlight and extend the foundation all the way up to the eyelashes.

5.

If you have real bags under the eyes, getting rid of them with a brush and some paint is almost impossible.

6.

To make your nose appear narrower, brush both sides with shading color. Avoid using extra highlight along the center—the side shading has created a highlighting effect already.

7–8.

Rouge is selected according to your foundation tone. If you are using cream rouge, apply it now, before powdering your face. Using a foam rubber sponge as an applicator, place your rouge directly below the cheekbone and blend it smoothly into the foundation. If you will be wearing cake rouge, however, you must apply it after you have powdered your face—as in step 21–22.

9.

When you are creating a three-dimensional face—bringing out the bone structure—a little highlight may be added directly below the rouge and blended down over the jawbone. Don't overdo this.

10.

Eyeshadow for a black woman should be closely related to the base foundation. Avoid using green, blue, or white unless dictated by the character. A three-dimensional look can be achieved by using highlight over the eyelid close to the eyelashes.

11.

A dark shade of eyeshadow should be used the rest of the way up to the eyebrows.

12.

Powder the entire face. Never rub—simply pat it on. Avoid dark brown powder, since it will change all the highlights and shadings you've already applied. Regular translucent powder is best.

13.

Brush off any excess powder.

14.

Using a very sharp eyebrow pencil and a feather stroke technique, fill in and shape the empty areas of your eyebrows.

10

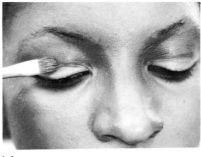

11

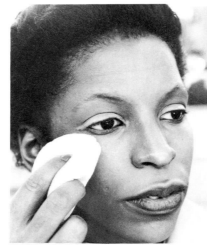

12

13

14

15

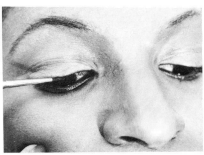

16

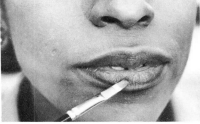

17

18

19

20

21

15–17.

Since liquid eyeliner flakes after it is dry and pencil lines eventually smear (creating a mess), it is advisable to use dark brown or black cake eyeliner with an eyeliner brush.

18.

A touch of pencil under the lower lashes, however, can frame your eyes beautifully—providing the line is not harsh or heavy.

19–20.

Choose the right shade of lipstick. And stay away from heavy lip gloss, as it will make your lips disappear. (On the other hand, a touch of lip gloss might be sufficient if your character has naturally colored lips.)

21.

At this time, if you think it is necessary, a touch of dry rouge can be applied here and there to create a natural effect (a touch on the forehead, over the chin, over the cream rouge you have already applied, and maybe under the eyebrows at the outer ends). Apply mascara on the upper and lower eyelashes. If it gets on your skin accidentally, remove it with a damp brush or Q-Tip—not your fingers or tissues—to prevent smudging.

22.

If you are using artificial eye-lashes, these should be cut to size unless already shaped. To shorten, cut off a small section and shape the rest. Usually the outer end of the strip is longer than the inner.

23.

A lash strip can be thinned and shaped by holding it in one hand and approaching the hairs at right angles with the tip of a scissors, making some shorter than others and snipping out unwanted hairs.

24.

Another way of shaping is to hold the lash strip against a table (strip side down) and, placing a razor blade at right angles to the seam, snip out a hair at a time.

25.

Apply a small amount of Duo surgical adhesive to the bonded end of the strip.

26.

Place the strip directly at the root of your eyelashes, touching the skin. Never place it on top of your own eyelashes or your eyelids.

27.

Press the lashes down with a toothpick, orange stick, or the end of a brush. Whichever you use, be careful. (A word of advice: whenever you're working on someone else's eyes, make sure the person's head is resting against the back of a chair.)

22

23   24

25

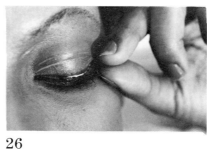

26

27

28

29

30

31

32

28.
If you prefer using individual eyelashes, take a pair of regular eyelashes and cut them with scissors or a razor, a few hairs at a time.

29.
Place a drop of Duo surgical adhesive on a clean surface.

30.
Lift each section of hairs with a tweezers and dip the end into adhesive.

31.
Gently place the hairs next to your own eyelashes—as far apart and as many as desired, depending on how thin or sparse your own lashes are.

32.
The final result should be a beautiful face that does not look made-up. Make sure your hands, neck, and arms are made up before leaving the makeup room.

If you choose the correct shade of foundation (one that matches your skin tone or is a shade or two darker), and if you apply it lightly and follow the steps as explained, you can appear in front of film and television cameras without any problems. In television it is important to stay away from colored eyeshadows (choose a shade near your foundation) and to select a lipstick without blue in its formula.

Straight Makeup for White Men

MATERIALS

1. Foundation
2. Foam rubber sponge
3. Highlight (a few shades lighter than the foundation)
4. Shading (a few shades darker than the foundation), if necessary
5. Two ⅜" brushes for highlight and shading
6. Cream and/or cake rouge
7. Translucent powder and puff
8. Eyebrow pencil (the color of your hair)
9. Comb and brush

For information on choosing the right foundation, the corresponding highlight and shadow, and, in fact, the whole style of makeup for the character you are portraying, read "Choice of Foundation" on page xii of the Introduction.

APPLICATION

1.

Begin with a clean face.

1

2.

Apply foundation with a foam rubber sponge. The shade you choose depends entirely on the age, living conditions, and general health of the character, not what you like or what you have in your makeup kit. A few shades can be mixed to achieve the right tone.

2

3.

Dark circles or discoloration under the eyes can be covered with highlight, depending on how dark the discoloration is. If highlight turns the skin under your eyes a grayish tone, however, eliminate it and extend your foundation all the way up to the eyelashes. A touch of red mixed with the foundation, such as Sunburn by Bob Kelly, can also be applied under the eyes to avoid this unwanted gray.

3

4.

If there are prominent pouches or bags under the eyes, little can be done—short of plastic surgery—to conceal them completely.

4

5

6

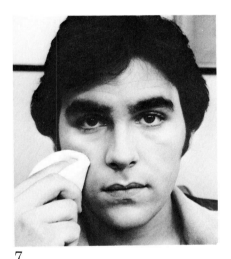

7

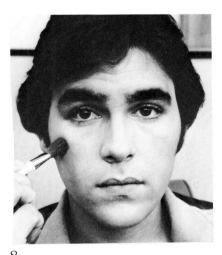

8

5.
There are two ways to apply rouge: cream rouge should be used now, before powdering your face; cake rouge should be applied after powdering.

6.
To conceal a fairly wide nose—when your character should have a thin one—use shading color on both sides. It is not necessary to use highlight down the center—the shading creates this effect naturally.

7.
Powder the entire face with translucent powder.

8–9.
Apply touches of cake rouge all over your face—mostly on the chin, cheekbone, and forehead, where sunshine usually hits first.

9

10–12.

If you have a receding or thinning hairline, fill in these areas with a very sharp eyebrow pencil (the same color as your hair)—just enough to achieve a natural look.

13.

The end result comes only after you brush and comb your hair, dress, and get into character. Make sure your hands are made up before leaving the makeup room.

The steps explained here are simply a guideline. For aid in other problem areas, read Chapter 1 on corrective makeup.

If you choose the correct shade of foundation (matching your skin tone), apply it lightly, and follow the steps explained here, you can appear in front of film and television cameras without any problems.

10

11

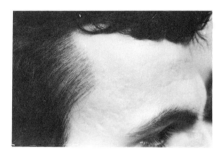
12

13

5

Straight Makeup for Black Men

MATERIALS

1. Foundation
2. Foam rubber sponge
3. Highlight (a few shades lighter than the foundation)
4. Shading (a few shades darker than the foundation), if necessary
5. Assorted brushes for blending and shading (two ⅜″ brushes; powder and rouge brushes)
6. Cream and/or cake rouge
7. Translucent powder and puff
8. Eyebrow pencil (the color of your hair)

For information on choosing the right foundation, the corresponding highlight and shadow, and, in fact, the whole style of makeup for the character you are portraying, read "Choice of Foundation" on page xii of the Introduction.

APPLICATION

1.

Begin with a clean face.

2.

Depending on the tone of your skin, choose a foundation that's a shade or two darker—preferably a warmer tone. Never use any makeup lighter than your own natural coloring (un-

1

2

less the character is to look "ashen"). It will appear gray and unnatural.

3.

Your face might have different tones in different areas. Using a foam rubber sponge as an applicator, spread an even shade all over. If you're mixing several colors to get the right shade, hold them in one hand and go over each one with the foam rubber sponge before applying.

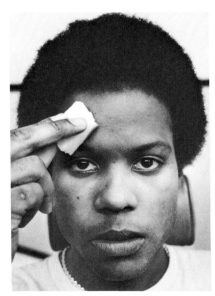

3

4.

Circles or discoloration under the eyes can be covered by applying a little highlight and blending it into the rest of the foundation. If there is too much of a contrast, eliminate the highlight and extend your foundation all the way up to the eyelashes.

5.

If you have prominent pouches or bags under your eyes, there is little chance—other than plastic surgery—of completely concealing them.

6–7.

At this point, depending on your skin tone, your face might need the addition of a little warm color. If so, take some rouge and gently go over the cheekbone, chin, and forehead to break the evenness and to create a more natural look.

4

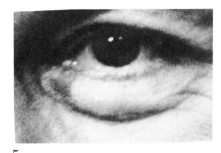

5

6

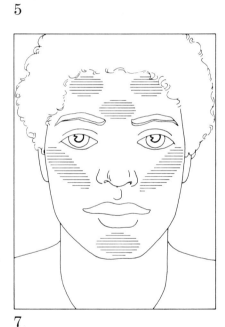

7

8.
If you wish to narrow your nose, apply shading color on either side. This will make it appear sharper.

9–10.
If this shading does not achieve the desired sharpness, apply a touch of highlight to the bridge of your nose. Make sure it doesn't look made-up and obvious.

11.
Powder your entire face. Since a dark powder that matches your skin will automatically cover all your natural shading and coloration, use translucent powder. Dab it on gently—do not rub.

8

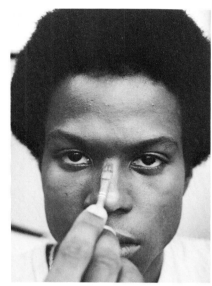

9

10

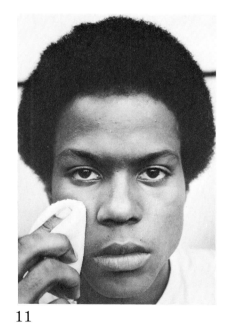

11

12.
Brush off the excess powder, if any.

13.
If your eyebrows or temple areas need filling in, do so by using a sharp eyebrow pencil. Draw individual lines and be careful not to smear them.

14.
To add more color at this point (or later on) you must use dry cake rouge and a rouge brush. Apply very gently. Make sure your hands are made up before leaving the makeup room.

15.
The final result.

For aid in other problem areas, read Chapter 1 on corrective makeup.

If you choose the correct shade of foundation, apply it lightly, and follow the steps explained here, you can appear in front of film and television cameras without any problems.

12

13

14

15

6

Middle Age Makeup for Women, Black or White

Applying middle age makeup is perhaps the hardest, since often the problem is to add only a few years of aging for the desired effect. For men, the addition of gray hair and a mustache can be a great help. For women, unless the muscle structure lends itself to subtle aging, it is necessary to let the proper hairstyle, costume, and "inner makeup" create the right age (see pp. xii–xii of the Introduction).

MATERIALS

1. Foundation
2. Foam rubber sponge
3. Shading (a few shades darker than the foundation)
4. Highlight (a few shades lighter than the foundation)
5. Assorted brushes (lipstick brush, two ⅜″ brushes for highlight and shading)
6. Translucent powder and puff
7. Eyebrow pencil
8. Lipstick

For information on choosing the right foundation, the corresponding highlight and shadow, and, in fact, the whole style of makeup for the character you are portraying, read "Choice of Foundation" on page xii of the Introduction.

Before you begin, examine your face in front of a mirror—either under an overhead light or simply by bending your head—and notice the areas where highlight and shadow could give the additional years needed.

There are two approaches for aging—whether middle-aged or older—for both blacks and whites. Either you can begin by adding highlights over the muscle structures of the face, or you can use shading under and around the muscle structures to make them stand out. Both of these approaches have a great deal to do with the skin tone you have selected for the character. White women with light skin tones should begin with shading as described in this chapter, while those with dark skin tones should begin with highlight as in Chapter 8. Black women with light skin tones should also begin with shading as described here; those with very dark skin tones should begin with highlight as described in Chapter 9.

1

APPLICATION

1.

Begin with a clean face. Then, using a foam rubber sponge, apply your foundation thinly and evenly. Avoid using a heavy foundation.

2–3.

Take your brush and gently add shading color to the circles, discoloration, or sunken areas around or under your eyes. Be extremely careful not to overdo this.

4–5.

You can also gently shade those depressed areas on either side of your nostrils.

6.

Carefully play with the areas at the corners of your mouth until you get the right three-dimensional look without appearing painted and old.

7.

If shading has not given you the right age, don't continue applying it (i.e., using too much in the process). Instead, try a cautious addition of highlight near the shadings and on prominent parts of the face.

8.

After you're sure you've done all you can, without going overboard, powder your entire face with translucent powder.

9.

Use a very sharp eyebrow pencil to fill in the empty spots in your eyebrows. If they are very light, darken the hairs gently.

10.

And, if you think it's necessary, you can emphasize any sunken areas around your eyes with a touch of eyebrow pencil.

2

3

4

5

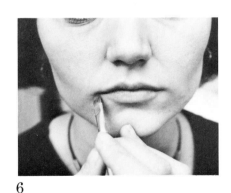

6

7

8

9

10

11

12

11–12.

Lipstick, plus the right type of hairstyle and costume, should complete the process. Here I have chosen not to use mascara, eyeliner, or rouge. This does not mean, however, that your character should go without any. It depends on what she would choose. Make sure your hands and neck get the same treatment before you leave the makeup room.

No matter what kind of makeup you decide on, don't overdo it. It is so easy to look too old and out of character.

If you choose the right foundation for the character you are portraying, apply it lightly, and follow the steps taken here, you can also use it in front of film and television cameras.

Extreme care must be taken when using highlight and shadow. Otherwise you'll wind up looking made-up. Facial muscles must be followed and worked with. Avoid drawing arbitrary lines here and there, and avoid overdoing it. You can go only so far with this technique in film and television. Lighting and close-ups must be considered at all times. A good lighting designer can help you achieve this type of aging even more than anything you could do with highlight and shadow. In any case, always use as little makeup as possible; you can always add to it. Don't forget that the hairstyle, costume, and total physical adaptability are part of the whole aging process.

7

Middle Age Makeup for Men, Black or White

Middle age manifests itself either early or late in life, depending on your character's living conditions and his state of health. You must determine these factors before getting to work.

Each face has to be treated differently. Place yourself in front of a mirror, either under an overhead light or simply bending your head, and examine the highlights and shadows on your face. Then select a few areas that best serve you for creating middle age. It is easy to go overboard and look old. Several practice sessions are a good idea.

MATERIALS

1. Foundation
2. Foam rubber sponge
3. Shading (usually a few shades darker than the foundation)
4. Highlight (usually a few shades lighter than the foundation), if necessary
5. Assorted brushes (toothbrush or eyebrow brush, two ⅜″ brushes)
6. Hair whitener, liquid or stick
7. Translucent powder and puff
8. Pair of mustaches

For information on choosing the right foundation, the corresponding highlight and shadow, and, in fact, the whole style of makeup for the character you are portraying, read "Choice of Foundation" on page xii of the Introduction.

There are two approaches for aging —whether middle-aged or older—for both blacks and whites. Either you can begin by adding highlights over the muscle structures of the face, or you can use shading under and around the muscle structures to make them stand out. Both of these approaches have a great deal to do with the skin tone you have selected for the character. White men with light skin tones should begin with shading as described in this chapter, while those with dark skin tones should begin with highlight as in Chapter 8. Black men with light skin tones should also begin with shading as described here; those with very dark skin tones should begin with highlight as described in Chapter 9.

APPLICATION

1.

Begin with a clean face. Then, using a foam rubber sponge as an applicator, apply your foundation thinly and evenly. Avoid using a heavy foundation.

2–3.

Take your brush and use shading to emphasize the dark shadows, circles, or discoloration under the eyes. In most cases this area, if it exists, has a purplish tone.

1

2

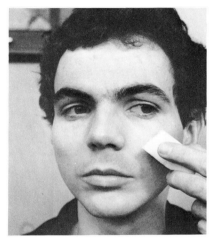

3

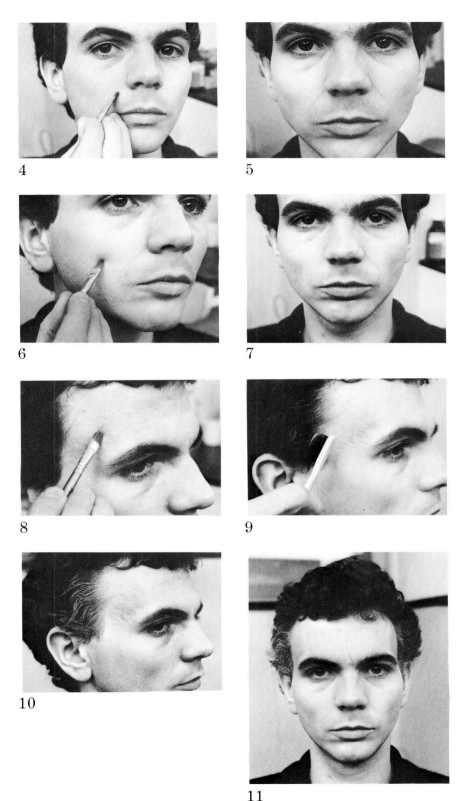

4

5

6

7

8

9

10

11

4–5.
The lines under the nasolabial folds should be emphasized.

6–7.
Accentuate the area under the cheekbone, creating what is known as "hollow cheeks." This step does not work on all faces. (If you have very healthy, round cheeks, for example, you will only wind up with a dirty face.)

8.
For a "lean" look, the temple areas can be darkened. If shading has not given you the right age, however, don't continue applying it (i.e., using too much in the process). Instead, try a cautious addition of highlight near the shadings and on prominent parts of the face.

9–11.
Graying the hair at the temples and sideburns—and perhaps, very slightly, at the widow's peak—will help create a sense of age. Hair whiteners are available in liquid and stick form, and come in white, yellow, and light blue-gray colors. Do not use the white or silver spray, since the former will give a metallic cast to your hair and the latter a bluish tone. Use either yellow or blue-gray M22B.

12–13.

"Before" and "after." The addition of a mustache definitely creates the best result—if it is in keeping with your character. Make sure your hands and neck get the same treatment before you leave the makeup room.

You might use all or some of these steps, but whatever you decide on, don't overdo it. It is so easy to look too old and out of character.

If you choose the right foundation for the character you are portraying, apply it lightly, and follow the steps taken here, you can also use it in front of film and television cameras.

Extreme care must be taken when using highlight and shadow. Otherwise you'll wind up looking made-up. Facial muscles must be followed and worked with. Avoid drawing arbitrary lines here and there, and avoid overdoing it. You can go only so far with this technique in film and television. Lighting and close-ups must be considered at all times. A good lighting designer can help you achieve this type of aging even more than anything you could do with highlight and shadow. In any case, always use as little makeup as possible; you can always add to it.

If you are using a chin beard, remember that the lace must be extremely fine. This can be covered, if necessary, with extra matching hairs to give a more natural look. If you are laying on a beard, the edges must look neat and clean, and the top layers must be sparse and lighter than the lower ones.

Don't forget that the hairstyle, costume, and total physical adaptability are part of the whole aging process.

12

13

8

Aging the Face and Hands with Highlight and Shadow

Aging the Face

MATERIALS

1. Foundation
2. Foam rubber sponge
3. Highlight (a few shades lighter than the foundation)
4. Shading (a few shades darker than the foundation)
5. Assorted brushes (toothbrush or eyebrow brush, two ⅜″ brushes for blending)
6. Dark brown eyebrow pencil
7. Translucent powder and puff
8. Hair whitener, liquid or stick

For information on choosing the right foundation, the corresponding highlight and shadow, and, in fact, the whole style of makeup for the character you are portraying, read "Choice of Foundation" on page xii of the Introduction.

APPLICATION

1.

Apply foundation all over your face, using a foam rubber sponge as an applicator.

2–5.

Make faces at yourself in front of a mirror to find your frown lines, crow's feet, and forehead and neck lines.

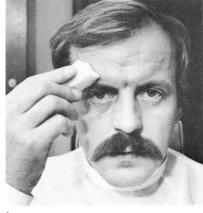

1

2

3

4

5

6–8.

If you have an overhead light, stand directly under it. Turn other lights off and observe the highlights and shadows on your face. Or, simply bend your head and look in the mirror—you will clearly see the areas that must be brought out with highlight as well as the areas that must be diminished with shading.

9.

Begin the process of aging by gently lifting your forehead and placing a highlight brush inside the creases. Then pull the brush down vertically. Continue doing this, section by section, until all prominent areas of your face contain highlight.

10.

Gently smooth out the highlighted areas, leaving certain areas lighter than others. Then examine your face in the mirror. Depending on the tone of your base, highlight alone might give you the aging needed. If not, follow the next step.

11.

After dipping a clean, ⅜″ brush into shading color, place its flat tip next to a highlighted area and brush upwards. Each intense area of highlight should be next to an intense area of dark shading. Since every fold and muscle catches light and casts a shadow in a different way, some will be sharp and straight, some round, and some long or oblong. When you are satisfied with what you have done, smooth out the shadings and the job is completed.

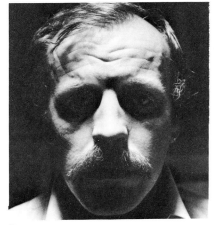

6

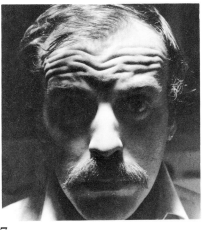

7

8

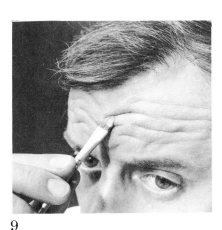

9

10

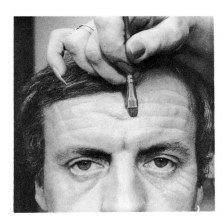

11

12

13

14

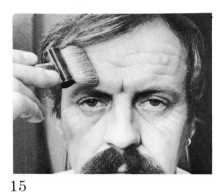

15

16

17

18

12–13.

If extra depth is needed in certain areas of wrinkles, try using a dark brown pencil with a sharp tip. Make sure, however, that the lines do not look "drawn."

14.

Powder the entire face with translucent powder. *Do not rub*; just pat gently.

15.

Brush off excess powder, if necessary.

16.

For the age you have created, it might be necessary now to add some gray hair or a gray mustache. Hair whiteners are available in liquid and stick form, and come in white, yellow, and light blue-gray colors. Do not use the white or silver spray, since the former will give a metallic cast to your hair and the latter a bluish tone. Use either yellow or blue-gray M22B, making sure the thickness of the hair is penetrated, not just the surface. Gray your eyebrows and hair, but not your eyelashes. For eyelashes, simply add some of the foundation color.

17–18.

"Before" and "after." Look in the mirror. If your makeup looks like makeup, you need more practice. If it looks natural, you're moving in the right direction.

If you need further aging, read Chapter 11. Do not forget to age your hands.

Aging the Hands

The procedure used here corresponds to that used for the face.

MATERIALS

1. Foundation
2. Foam rubber sponge
3. Highlight (a few shades lighter than the foundation)
4. Shading (a few shades darker than the foundation)
5. Assorted brushes (three ¼" brushes and a rouge brush)
6. Blue-gray lining color
7. Cream or powdered rouge
8. Translucent powder and puff

APPLICATION

1.
Apply the basic foundation using a foam rubber sponge as an applicator.

2.
Hold your hand under direct overhead light. Move it around until you see all the bones, veins, and muscle structures created by highlight and shadow.

3.
With a clean brush apply highlights on all prominent parts of your hand, as observed under the light.

4.
Take another brush and darken all the shaded or depressed areas next to the highlighted ones.

5.
Shade the areas between the knuckles on both sides of each finger.

6.
To bring out the natural wrinkles on the knuckles, bend your fingers and apply a touch of shading color over each knuckle.

1

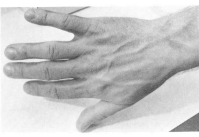

2

3

4

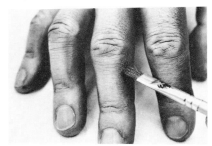

5

6

7–8.

Spread your fingers and go over the wrinkles, emphasizing them with a light touch of highlight.

9.

A touch of blue-gray over the veins will make them more prominent.

10.

If you have cream rouge, the time to apply it is now, before powdering. A touch over each knuckle is a great help in creating aged hands.

11.

If you have cake rouge, powder your hands and then apply cake rouge over the knuckles with a piece of cotton or a rouge brush. Be extremely careful not to wash your hands, rub them together, or put them into your pockets. This applies to any technique you might use for aging hands.

12.

The end result.

If you choose the right foundation for the character you are portraying, apply it lightly, and follow the steps taken here, you can also use it in front of film and television cameras.

Extreme care must be taken when using highlight and shadow. Otherwise you'll wind up looking made-up. Facial muscles must be followed and worked with. Avoid drawing arbitrary lines here and there, and avoid overdoing it. You can go only so far with this technique in film and television. Lighting and close-ups must be considered at all times. A good lighting

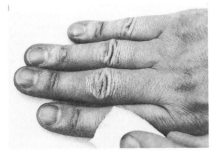

7

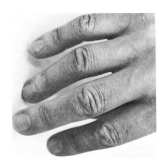

8

9

10

11

designer can help you achieve this type of aging even more than anything you could do with highlight and shadow. In any case, always use as little makeup as possible; you can always add to it. Don't forget that the hairstyle, costume, and total physical adaptability are part of the whole aging process.

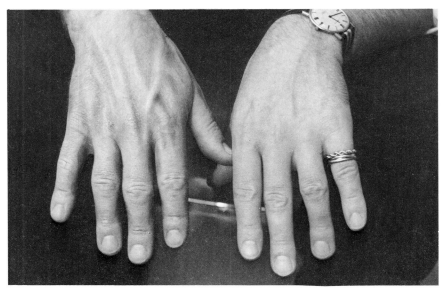

12

9

Aging with Highlight and Shadow for Very Dark Black Men or Women

The basic principle governing aging with highlight and shadow is to darken the depressed areas of the muscle and bone structures, bringing out the prominent areas with highlight. If a black person has light skin, this should not be difficult, and the step by step approach in Chapter 8 can be followed. If the skin is really black, however, there is no way to darken the depressed areas. In such cases aging must be approached in a "negative" way, using only highlight and leaving the actual skin tone as the shading.

MATERIALS

1. Foundation (one shade or a combination of several)
2. Foam rubber sponge
3. Highlight (a few shades lighter than the foundation)
4. Assorted brushes (toothbrush or eyebrow brush, and two ⅜″ brushes for highlight and shading)
5. Translucent powder and puff
6. Black eyebrow pencil
7. Hair whitener, liquid or stick

1

2

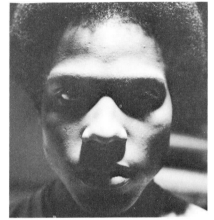

3

4

5

For information on choosing the right foundation, the corresponding highlight and shadow, and, in fact, the whole style of makeup for the character you are portraying, read "Choice of Foundation" on page xii of the Introduction.

APPLICATION

1.
Begin with a clean face.

2.
If your skin tone, though very dark, is uneven, use the same

shade of foundation as the darkest part of your skin. Apply it evenly all over your face and neck, using a foam rubber sponge as an applicator.

3–5.
Now look in the mirror and examine your face—either under an overhead light or simply by bending your head—noting the depressed areas and the pronounced ones. Wrinkle your forehead. Smile and frown. Each expression will show where to apply highlight.

6–7.
Take a ⅜″ brush and begin by applying highlights as you see them on your face. This must be done carefully to avoid smearing.

8.
Now smooth and blend the edges. After a while you'll begin to see the age.

9.
When you're satisfied, use translucent powder to take away the shine. Pat, don't rub. And *don't* use dark powder—it will cover all your highlight and shading.

10–11.
If you think—after looking in the mirror while standing several feet away—that you need more depth here and there, use a black eyebrow pencil and deepen the lines. Don't overdo it.

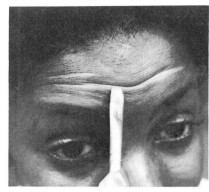

6

7

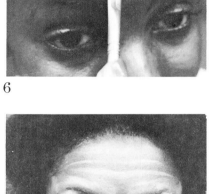

8

9

10

11

12.

If the age you have created now requires gray hair, apply hair whitener (in stick or liquid form) using an eyebrow brush or a toothbrush. For the right effect, don't just gray the surface—go deeper down for a natural look. And don't use white or silver spray; the former gives a metallic cast to your hair and the latter a bluish tone. The best colors are yellow or blue-gray M22B.

13–14.

When you've finished, bear in mind that the highlighted area, whatever shade it may be, is your new skin tone. Any part of your body that is seen, therefore, has to be changed to match this new shade. Make sure your hands and neck get the same aging treatment before leaving the makeup room.

If you choose the right foundation for the character you are portraying, apply it lightly, and follow the steps taken here, you can also use it in front of film and television cameras.

Extreme care must be taken when using highlight and shadow. Otherwise you'll wind up looking made-up. Facial muscles must be followed and worked with. Avoid drawing arbitrary lines here and there, and avoid overdoing it. You can go only so far with this technique in film and television. Lighting and close-ups must be considered at all times. A good lighting designer can help you achieve this type of aging even more

than anything you could do with highlight and shadow. In any case, always use as little makeup as possible; you can always add to it. Don't forget that the hairstyle, costume, and total physical adaptability are part of the whole aging process.

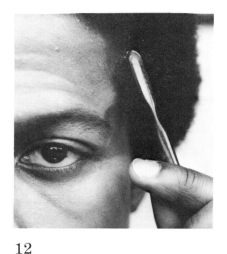

12

13 A

13 B

14 A

14 B

10

Aging with Liquid Latex for Men or Women, Black or White

Aging the Face

MATERIALS

1. Liquid latex or Duo surgical adhesive
2. Foam rubber sponge
3. Hand hair dryer
4. Translucent powder and puff
5. Rubber mask grease
6. Red-A in rubber mask grease or stick
7. Acrylic paints, mixed with latex to match the foundation
8. Hair whitener, liquid or stick
9. Toothbrush or eyebrow brush
10. Stipple sponge
11. Red-A, Green, and Yellow Creme Stick

For information on choosing the right foundation, the corresponding highlight and shadow, and, in fact, the whole style of makeup for the character you are portraying, read "Choice of Foundation" on page xii of the Introduction.

For this makeup it is absolutely necessary to have someone help you. Before doing anything, however, plan your entire work in your mind or write it down. There are ten sections you have to cover: forehead,

eyelids, both sides of the face, upper lip (if you don't have a mustache), chin, lower lip, neck, and nose. All sections must overlap each other.

In the application of liquid latex, any area of the face you pull horizontally (from both sides) will give you vertical wrinkles, and any area you pull vertically will give you horizontal wrinkles.

APPLICATION

1.

Begin with a clean face. Using a foam rubber sponge as an applicator, quickly apply a generous layer of liquid latex all over your forehead, as close as possible to (but not in) your eyebrows and hairline. If you don't move fast enough and are not generous enough, the latex will dry before the next step.

2.

Putting one hand over your eyebrows, pull them down as far as you can without touching the wet latex; with your other hand, pull your hair back as far as you can. While holding your forehead this way, have someone dry it with a hand hair dryer. When the latex dries it becomes colorless and transparent. Keep the tension while another generous latex layer is being added. Dry this layer, too.

3.

Keep the pull and tension while your entire forehead is being powdered. *Do not* release it before powdering.

1

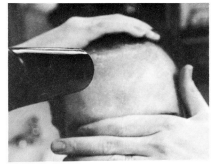

2

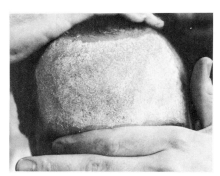

3

4.

Now relax and move your eyebrows up and down a few times—the new wrinkles will fall into place. Depending on the flexibility of your skin, you will get small or large wrinkles. Don't expect miracles.

5.

Pull the eyebrow up with one hand and the eyelid down with the other (place the tip of your finger on your eyelashes—if you are doing it yourself just pull the eyebrow up, keeping your eye closed, and with a small piece of foam rubber sponge apply a generous layer of liquid latex over your eyelid without getting it in your eyelashes or eyebrows). Dry with a hand hair dryer. When dry, add a second layer without releasing the skin. Dry again, powder, then relax.

6–7.

Do the same with the other eyelid. The flexibility determines the amount of wrinkles you'll get. If you pull up the center of the eyebrows, you'll get unnatural horizontal wrinkles. It's better, therefore, to pull up the outer edge for diagonal and more natural wrinkles.

8–9.

For the sides of the face apply a generous layer of liquid latex, as fast as possible, to cover the area shown in the picture. Stretch the skin in both directions, then hold and dry. Add a second coat while stretching the skin. Dry and powder. Then relax and move your muscles for the wrinkles to fall into place. Make sure the tips of your fingers are not touching the latex;

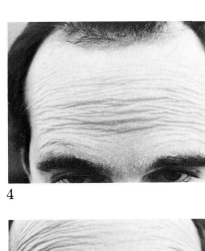
4

5

6

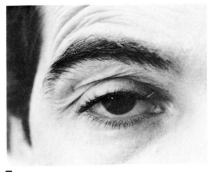
7

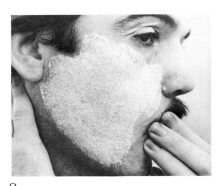
8

9

if they are, you'll have trouble lifting your fingers without also lifting off the edges of the latex. (It would be safer to dip your fingers in powder.)

10.
Follow the same directions for the other side of your face.

11–13.
Apply the same generous amount of liquid latex on the upper lip, if you don't have a mustache. Dry, then add a second layer of latex. Dry again, powder, and relax. Do the same with the chin and lower lip. (Since you have to place your fingers over the sides of your face to pull back the skin, it is advisable to dip your fingers in powder beforehand. This prevents any damages that might otherwise occur.)

14.
Apply one coat of latex on your nose, overlapping the other sections. Dry and powder. Since you cannot wrinkle your nose, no stretching is necessary. The reason for this application is to give your nose the same texture as the rest of your face.

10

11

12

13

14

15–17.

To do your neck it is necessary to bend your head as far back as possible and stay in this position until finished. Apply a generous layer of liquid latex, as shown in the picture. Dry, hold, and add a second layer. Dry again, hold, and powder. Then relax.

18.

Now look in the mirror. If you've missed certain areas—such as your temples and neck, especially towards the back, and under your eyes—apply a small amount of liquid latex so these areas conform with the rest of your face.

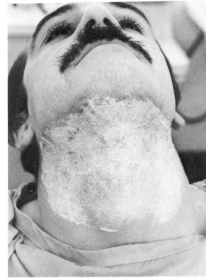

15

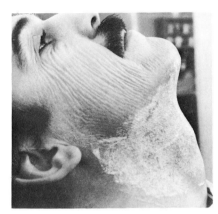

16

17

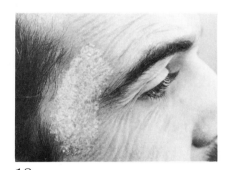

18

19.

Using a foam rubber sponge as an applicator, apply a thin coat of rubber mask grease all over your face and neck. To prevent rubber mask grease from rubbing on shirt or dress collars, color the neck areas by mixing several shades of acrylic paint with liquid latex until the latex matches the foundation. Stipple this new mixture on the neck area, or all over the face if you want to. If you cannot mix the right shade of foundation with acrylic paints, try one or two complete layers of regular liquid latex. Dry the latex without stretching it. Do not color or powder—the sheen adds a nice effect.

20–21.

For the old age you have created, gray hair, a mustache, and perhaps eyebrows are necessary—unless specified otherwise in the script. There are a few shades of hair whitener available in liquid or stick form, such as yellow or blue M22B. Do not use white or silver spray. The former makes your hair metallic and the latter gives it a bluish tone.

Place a small eyebrow brush or an old toothbrush at the root of the hair and move up, making sure each hair is completely grayed. Let it dry and then comb gently. For eyelashes, simply add some of the foundation color.

19

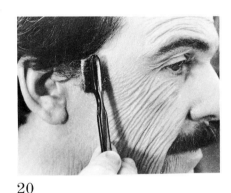

20

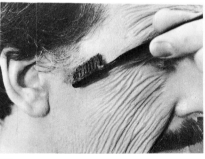

21

22.

If you find that your makeup looks flat, take a Red-A Creme Stick and a sponge for stippling and texture your face. I even add a gentle touch of green and yellow, which is present in every face. All this coloring, however, should not interfere with the character you are portraying. Follow his dictates, according to his state of health and environment.

23–25.

If necessary, "liver spots" or different-sized moles can be added here and there. For the liver spots, mix several colors together to achieve a brownish-purple; then brush this onto your face in various places. For the moles, scatter a few droplets of liquid latex over a table or mirror, let them dry overnight, and then glue them to your face with a touch of liquid latex. Color them if desired. (For more information on liver spots and moles, see Chapter 28, Odds and Ends.) Gently powder your face, dust it off, and look in the mirror.

22

23

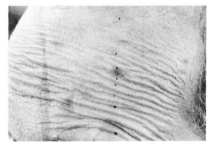

24

25

26

27

26–27.
"Before" and "after." If the end result looks like a made-up face, you need more practice. If it looks natural, as it should, you're heading in the right direction.

Aging with Liquid Latex for a Black Female Performer

1–4.

Follow steps 1–19 of this chapter; only the foundation color and corresponding highlight and shadow will be different.

If the age you have created now requires gray hair, apply hair whitener (in stick or liquid form) using an eyebrow brush or an old toothbrush. Don't just gray the surface; go deeper down for a natural look. And don't use white or silver spray. The former gives your hair a metallic cast; the latter gives it a bluish tone. The best colors are yellow or blue-gray M22B. For eyelashes, simply add some of the foundation color.

1

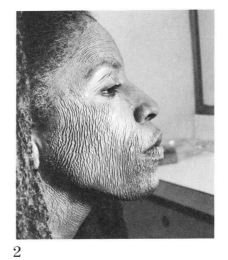

2

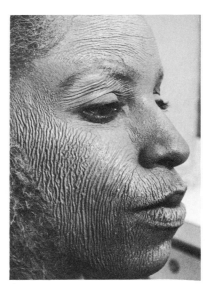

3

4

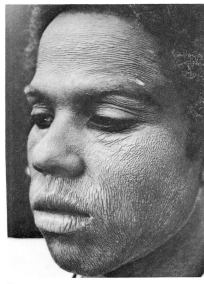

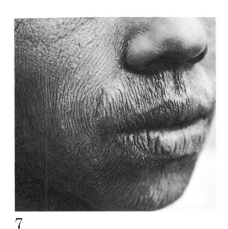

5

6

7

8

Aging with Liquid Latex for a Black Male Performer

5–8.
Follow steps 1-19 of this chapter; only the foundation color and corresponding highlight and shadow will be different.

If the age you have created now requires gray hair, apply hair whitener (in stick or liquid form) using an eyebrow brush or an old toothbrush. Don't just gray the surface; go deeper down for a natural look. And don't use white or silver spray. The former gives your hair a metallic cast; the latter gives it a bluish tone. The best colors are yellow or blue-gray M22B. For eyelashes, simply add some of the foundation color.

Aging the Hands

This technique corresponds to the face aged with liquid latex.

MATERIALS

1. Liquid latex
2. Foam rubber sponge
3. Translucent powder and puff
4. Hand hair dryer
5. Rubber mask grease
6. Red, pink, and blue-gray lining colors
7. Assorted brushes (¼″, ⅜″)

APPLICATION

1.

Using a foam rubber sponge as an applicator, apply a generous amount of liquid latex to the backs of your hands, fingers, and wrists. This must be done as fast as possible, since it dries very quickly. Pat—do not rub—for the best results.

2.

Curl your fingers and bend your wrist. Keep this position until your hands are completely powdered. Make sure all your fingers are separated.

3.

Dry with a hand hair dryer. When the liquid latex becomes totally transparent (keep your fingers curled), add another generous layer of latex and dry.

4.

Keeping the fingers curled, powder the entire area.

5.

Stretch your hand, then close it and open your fingers a few times so the new wrinkles can fall into place.

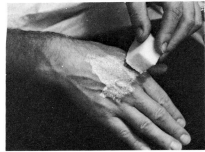

1

2

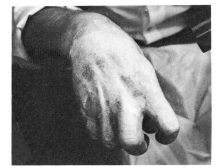

3

4

5

6–7.

Now turn your hands over and apply one or two latex layers to the palms. This will connect the back sections to the front. It will all seem like you're wearing thin latex gloves, and the chances of the edges peeling or lifting will be minimal—but not altogether avoidable, depending on how much you will be using your hands. To repair any area, apply some liquid latex on top, dry, and powder.

8.

Apply rubber mask grease, the same shade as the foundation. Before powdering you can add some red or pink coloring to the knuckles. The veins can also be emphasized and liver spots added. Then powder.

9.

The result depends entirely on the flexibility of your skin. The looser it is, the more wrinkles you will get.

To prevent rubber mask grease from rubbing on your clothes, follow the explanation in step 18 of this chapter.

If you are planning to use this makeup for television and film, take time to make sure that all layers are nicely overlapped, and that there are no rolled-up latex edges or unnatural lumps. It's also important to get as close to the hairline as possible without latex getting into it. If you're adding highlights and shadows over the latex, make sure they're well blended—your coloring should not be dull or shiny. Above all, be ready to make repairs when necessary around the mouth and the edges of your makeup, especially on your fingers and the areas of the neck where your clothes come in contact with the latex.

Remember that makeup by itself is not the answer to any characterization. You must consider that the hairstyle, costume, and total physical adaptability are part of the whole aging process.

6

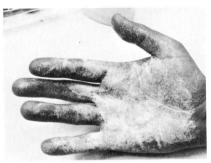

7

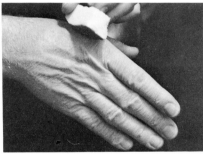

8

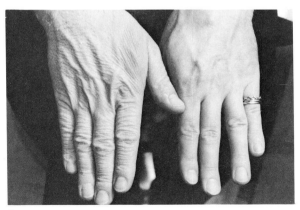

9

11

Aging with Kleenex for Men or Women, Black or White

Aging the Face

For this technique you will need someone to help you.

MATERIALS

1. Kleenex tissues
2. Liquid latex or Duo surgical adhesive
3. Foam rubber sponge
4. Hand hair dryer
5. Translucent powder and puff
6. Rubber mask grease
7. Red-A, Green, and Yellow Creme Stick
8. Stipple sponge
9. Hair whitener, liquid or stick
10. Toothbrush or eyebrow brush
11. Acrylic paints, mixed with latex to match the foundation

For information on choosing the right foundation, the corresponding highlight and shadow, and, in fact, the whole style of makeup for the character you are portraying, read "Choice of Foundation" on page xii of the Introduction.

APPLICATION

Divide your face into eight different sections—forehead, upper eyelids, left side of the face, right side of the face, upper lip (without mustache), neck, chin and lower lip, nose. Do each section separately, making sure the edges overlap.

1

1.

Each Kleenex tissue is two-ply. You need one single ply for each section.

2

2–3.

If you tear Kleenex tissues lengthwise, they rip straight down. They will not tear straight across the width. Prepare your tissues before continuing.

All applications should be made by laying down the tissue lengthwise—except on the chin and lower and upper lips. Remember: any area of the face that you pull (from both sides) horizontally will give you vertical wrinkles, and any area you pull vertically will give you horizontal wrinkles.

3

4.

Begin with a clean face. Using a foam rubber sponge as an applicator, apply a generous amount of liquid latex over the forehead, as close as possible to the hairline and eyebrows without getting it into the hair.

4

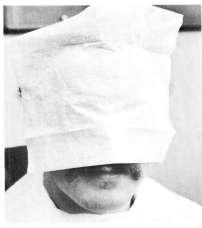

5

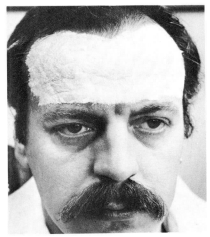

6

7

8

5–6.

While still wet, place one ply of Kleenex lengthwise over the latex and press to hold. After carefully cutting the excess overhanging tissue, saturate the remaining section with a generous layer of liquid latex.

7.

Placing one hand over your hair and one hand over your eyebrows, pull in opposite directions while someone dries your forehead with a hand hair dryer. Next, have your helper powder the entire area before you release your hands. Move your eyebrows up and down to set the new wrinkles. You'll get different types of wrinkles depending on the flexibility of your muscles and skin. (Make sure the tips of your fingers are not touching the latex; if they are, you'll have trouble lifting your fingers without also lifting all the edges of the latex. It would be safer to dip your fingers in powder.)

8.

Repeat the same technique on the upper eyelids, one at a time. Before you begin, cut the tissues the size of your eyelids.

9.

Pull the eyebrow up with one hand while placing the other hand on your eyelashes and pulling down. Dry, powder, and then let go of the tension.

10.

If you have any difficulty in applying tissues on your eyelids, you can use latex alone by applying it over the eyelid (using a very small foam rubber sponge as an applicator), as long as you're careful not to get any in your eyebrows or eyelashes. Pull as above. Dry. While you are holding the eyelid, your helper should add another layer. Dry again and powder before letting go of the tension.

11.

For the sides of the face, apply a generous amount of latex. Stay away from the hairline.

12.

Place the tissue on the face and press to hold.

13–14.

Cut the excess overhanging tissue, saturate the remaining section with liquid latex, and pull the face in opposite directions, being careful not to place your hands over the wet latex. Dry and powder, then release. Do the same on the other side.

9

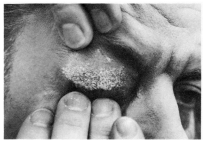

10

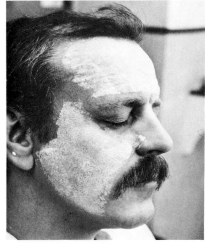

11

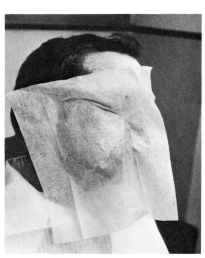

12

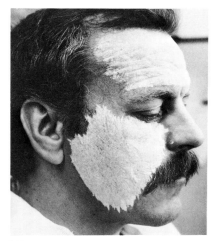

13

14

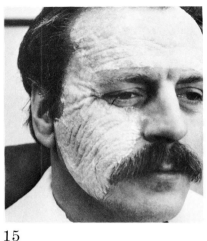

15

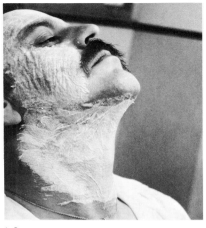

16

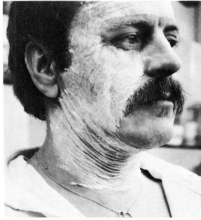

17

18

19

20

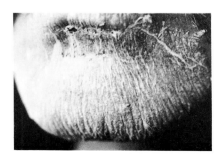

21

15.

If there are sections between the forehead and the sides of the face without Kleenex, such as the temple area, add a small piece on either side to connect the two sections.

16–17.

It is best if the neck is done in one session. Keeping your head up as far as you can, saturate the entire neck area with liquid latex. This must be done quickly or the latex will dry. Immediately lay on the Kleenex tissues, cut the excess, saturate the area again, dry, powder, and bring your head down.

(If you cannot do this in one section, divide the neck area into two or more horizontal sections and do each separately. Make sure that the position of the neck does not change and that all the edges overlap.)

To protect your clothing from rubber mask grease while coloring the neck area, mix a few shades of acrylic paint with liquid latex until it matches the foundation. Stipple this mixture on the neck area or all over the face if you like. If you cannot match the foundation with acrylic paint, substitute one or two complete layers of regular latex. Dry the latex without stretching it. Do not color or powder—the sheen adds a nice effect.

18–21.

The same technique applies to the chin and lower lip, except that here the tissues must be placed across the width, not lengthwise. Don't let go until the areas are dried and powdered, and don't forget to overlap.

22.

Though you can't wrinkle your nose, it should also be covered with Kleenex so the texture matches the rest of the face.

After all areas are finished, cover the entire face with a layer of rubber mask grease, mixing a shade appropriate to your character.

After the base, add a touch of Red-A Creme Stick all over, using a stipple sponge to make it more lively; or stipple a little yellow, red, and green here and there to give the entire face a natural look rather than a mask-like appearance.

Powder the entire face.

Gray the hair, eyebrows, and mustache, if any, using hair whitener and a toothbrush. Hair whiteners are available in liquid and stick form, and come in white, yellow, and light blue-gray colors. Don't use the white or silver spray, since the former gives your hair a metallic cast and the latter a bluish tone. Use either yellow or blue-gray M22B. For eyelashes, simply add some of the foundation color.

23–24.

"Before" and "after."

This makeup can be removed by soaking the entire face, neck, and hands in warm water and pulling it off very gently. You'll find that your skin will retain the impression of the wrinkles. Do not be alarmed—this condition is only temporary. After a few minutes your skin will return to its original youthfulness.

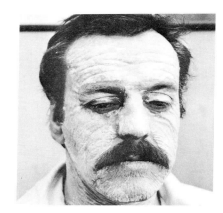

22

23

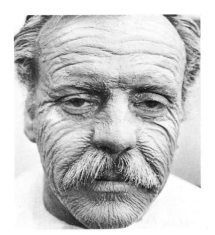

24

Aging with Kleenex for a Black Female Performer

A, B, C.

Follow steps 1-22 of this chapter; only the foundation color and corresponding highlight and shadow will be different.

Although you can't wrinkle your nose, it should also be covered with Kleenex so the texture matches the rest of the face.

After all areas are finished, cover the entire face with a layer of rubber mask grease, mixing a shade appropriate to your character.

After the base, add a touch of Red-A Creme Stick all over, using a stipple sponge to make it more lively.

Powder the entire face.

If the age you have created now requires gray hair and eyebrows, apply hair whitener (in stick or liquid form) using an eyebrow brush or an old toothbrush. Do not use the white or silver spray. The former gives your hair a metallic cast and the latter a bluish one. Use either yellow or blue-gray M22B. For eyelashes, you may simply add some of the foundation color.

A

B

C

Aging the Hands

This technique corresponds to that used for the face.

MATERIALS

1. Kleenex tissues
2. Liquid latex
3. Foam rubber sponge
4. Hand hair dryer
5. Translucent powder and puff
6. Rubber mask grease
7. Highlight

APPLICATION

1.

Separate two-ply Kleenex tissue, using one ply for each hand. Apply a generous layer of latex all over the back of the hand, fingers, and wrist (as quickly as possible or it will dry before the next step), using a foam rubber sponge as an applicator. Pat, don't rub.

2.

Before the latex dries, curl your fingers, palm, and wrist. Place the Kleenex on top and press hard until the latex comes through.

3.

Straighten your fingers and split or cut the excess tissues, exposing your nails.

4–5.

Apply another generous layer of liquid latex, saturating the Kleenex. While it's wet, tuck all the loose ends under and around the fingers and palm of your hand. Bend your wrist, then curl your fingers and palm, keeping your fingers separate. Dry the hand with a hair dryer.

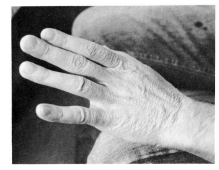

1

2

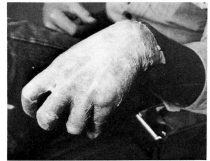

3

4

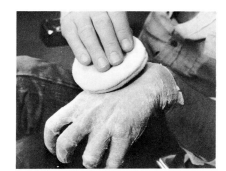

5

6

6.

Hold the form of your hand and powder it. Then cover the palm of your hand and fingers with liquid latex, dry, and powder again. This will create a thin latex glove. Although the chance of curling and lifting is minimal, it is not altogether avoidable.

7.

Color with rubber mask grease the same shade as the foundation.

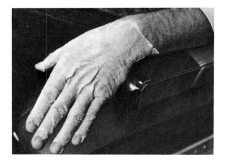

7

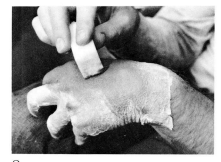

8

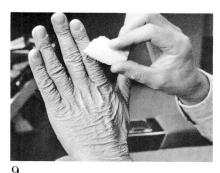

9

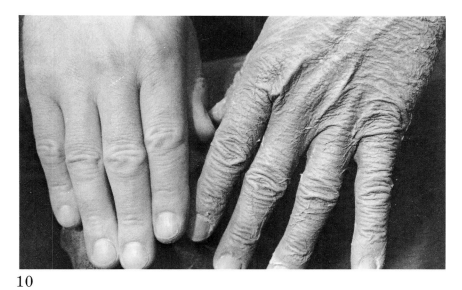

10

8-9.

If you want the newly created wrinkles to stand out more, choose a darker shade of rubber mask grease. Apply as before, then stretch out your fingers and very gently go over the wrinkles with a touch of highlight. Powder, and you're ready. If the edges loosen during the performance, repair them with liquid latex.

To prevent rubber mask grease from rubbing on your clothes, follow the directions on page 59 in this chapter.

10.

The final result.

These techniques should not be used in television and film for the leading characters. The best results can be achieved by applying foam rubber (prosthetic) pieces. Makeup artists working in film and television have the know-how and technical facilities to accomplish this task. But if there's no other way, aging with Kleenex can be used as long as the makeup artist takes enough time to overlap the tissues, and if he concentrates on all the fine details around the eyes, hairline, mouth, and neck.

Remember that makeup by itself is not the answer to any characterization. You must consider that the hairstyle, costume, and total physical adaptability are part of the whole aging process.

A final word of caution: always be ready to repair edges around the mouth, fingers, and neckline where they come in contact with clothes and makeup.

12

Aging for Men or Women with a Combination of Highlight, Shadow, and Liquid Latex

Aging the Face

1

2

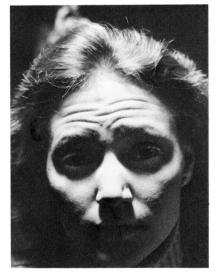

3

MATERIALS

1. Foundation (one shade or a combination of several shades)
2. Foam rubber sponge
3. Highlight (usually a few shades lighter than the foundation)
4. Shading (usually a few shades darker than the foundation)
5. Assorted brushes (two ⅜″ brushes for highlight and shadow, rouge, and lipstick)
6. Dark brown eyebrow pencil
7. Dry rouge
8. Lipstick
9. Translucent powder and puff
10. Hair whitener, liquid or stick
11. Liquid latex
12. Hand hair dryer
13. Latex eyebags (optional)
14. Tweezers

For information on choosing the right foundation, the corresponding highlight and shadow, and, in fact, the whole style of makeup for the character you are portraying, read "Choice of Foundation" on page xii of the Introduction.

APPLICATION

1.
Begin with a clean face.

2.
Apply foundation all over your face and neck, using a foam rubber sponge as an applicator. If you're mixing colors, hold them in one hand and gently pass the foam rubber sponge over each one before covering your face. Avoid using heavy foundation.

3.
If you're not familiar with the bone and muscle structure of your face, place yourself directly under an overhead light, or simply bend your head, and look in the mirror. Making faces is the best way to find out which areas to bring out with highlight and which to recede by shading.

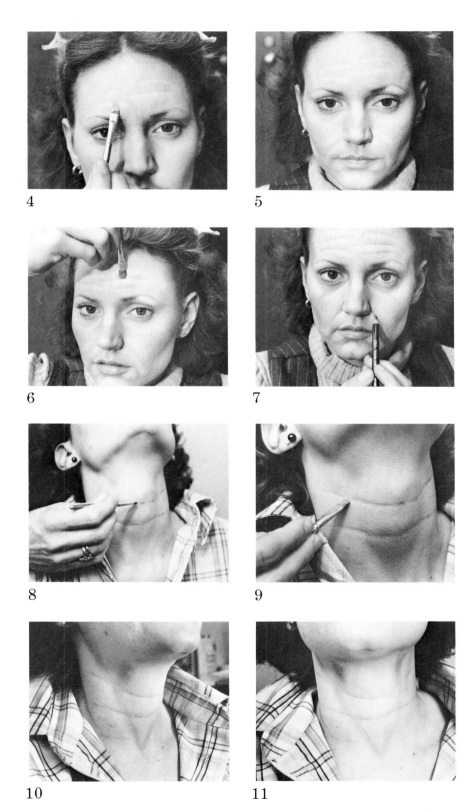

4

5

6

7

8

9

10

11

4.
Take a brush and apply highlights where they logically fall. For the forehead, begin by placing the tip of the brush in the center and gently pulling down. In other areas you might pull your brush sideways or around. Each fold and muscle catches light and casts shadows in different ways.

5.
Blend carefully without destroying the effect you have created.

6.
If the highlight alone does not give you the age you had in mind, shading should be applied under and around a highlighted muscle to bring it out and make it three-dimensional. Place your shading brush directly next to the highlight and move upward. The intense areas of highlight should be next to the intense shaded areas.

7.
If you want extra depth in certain areas—after smoothing, blending, and shaping the muscles—use a dark brown eyebrow pencil with a sharp point. Be very gentle.

8–11.
The same technique should be applied if your neck is going to show. Again, look in the mirror and take note of your natural lines. Simply bring out the prominent areas with highlight and, if necessary, add the shading as above.

12–13.

After you are totally satisfied with what you have done—and if you are not going to apply liquid latex for further aging—add a touch of rouge and lipstick, if the character does so; then powder your face and maybe gray your hair a bit with liquid or stick hair whitener, either yellow or blue-gray M22B. Do not use the white or silver spray. The former gives your hair a metallic cast, and the latter gives a bluish tone.

If you intend to apply liquid latex after the highlight and shadow, powder your face and begin the process of further aging. At this time it is advisable to have someone help you, since you will be using both hands.

Before you begin, remember this rule: any area of the face that is pulled horizontally from both sides will give vertical wrinkles, and any area that is pulled vertically will give horizontal wrinkles.

14.

Using a piece of foam rubber sponge as an applicator, spread a generous layer of liquid latex all over the forehead as close as possible to the hairline and eyebrows without getting any in the hair. You must do this quickly or it will dry before you begin the next step. Place one hand on your eyebrows to pull them down and the other on your hair to pull it back. Be careful not to smear the highlight and shadow. While you're pulling the skin, dry it with a hand hair dryer (someone can help you here).

12

13

14

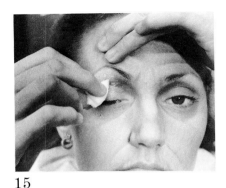

15

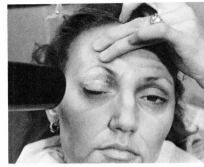

16

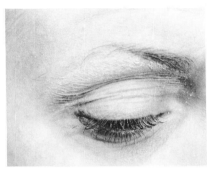

17

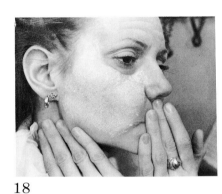

18

As soon as the liquid latex becomes transparent, add another layer of latex, continuing to pull the skin as you do. Then dry and powder—still pulling the skin—and then relax.

15–17.

Pull your eyebrow up and close your eye. (Or, if someone is helping you, use your other hand to pull down your eyelid.) Place your fingers on your eyelashes. Using a small piece of foam rubber sponge, apply a generous coat of liquid latex over the eyelid (one eye at a time). Be sure you don't get any in your eyelashes and eyebrows. Dry with a hand hair dryer. Hold the "pull" and add another layer of latex. Dry and powder (still pulling the skin), then release and relax. Depending on your muscle tone and skin condition, if you pull the eyebrows up from dead center you will get horizontal wrinkles, which are very unnatural. If you hold the outer end of the eyebrows and pull up, you will get more natural, diagonal wrinkles. Don't be disappointed if you're not getting a lot of wrinkles—or horrified if you are.

18.

Apply liquid latex on the side of the face, as shown. Use a generous amount and work as fast as possible. Pull your face first from one side and then from the other, and dry with a hand hair dryer. Make sure your fingers are not touching the latex. (It would be safer to dip your fingers in powder.) Then add a second layer while still pulling the skin. Dry, powder, and relax.

19.

You can apply latex to the upper lip, the lower lip, and the chin. Pull as shown, remembering to dip your fingers in the powder. Hold tightly. Dry. Add another layer and dry again. Then apply powder and release.

20–22.

Until you're finished, hold your chin up as high as possible to stretch your neck muscles. Apply a coat of liquid latex, working quickly, and then dry. Add a second layer and dry again. Powder and release.

23.

One coat of liquid latex on your nose gives it the same texture as the rest of your face.

24–25.

If you wish to create bags under your eyes, latex eyebags can be purchased. Apply a touch of liquid latex to the back of each eyebag and place them gently under your eyes using a tweezers. Press down until they hold.

26.

Apply a thin coat of latex over both eyebags. Dry and powder.

27–28.

Decide in advance whether or not to use eyebags. You can see the difference in these pictures.

Do not cover your liquid latex face with any other color. If you do, you will hide all the aging you've accomplished with highlight and shadow. (If your face looks "powdery," go over it sparingly with a damp sponge to let the highlight and shadow come through. Or, instead of

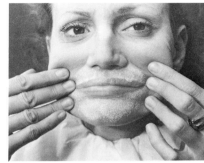

19

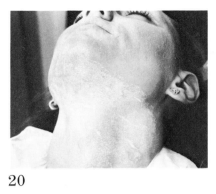

20

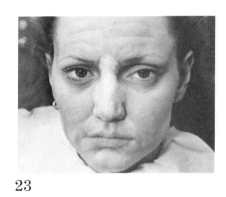

21

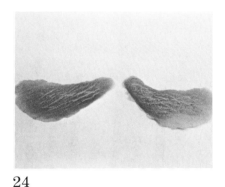

22

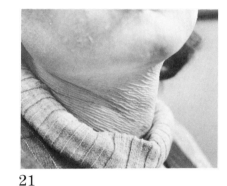

23

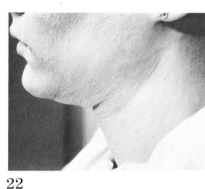

24

25

26

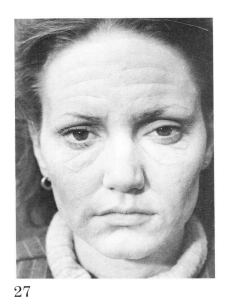

27

28

29

30

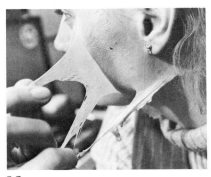

31   32

water, use castor oil with a brush or your finger as an applicator; this will give the face its natural sheen.)

29–30.
"Before" and "after."

31–32.
To remove this makeup, soak your face with damp, warm towels. Then, after a few minutes, wash with soap and water —the latex will peel off. If you try peeling your face without soaking and washing first, you're liable to pull the hair or "peach fuzz," which can be painful. Just be careful.

The aging of your hands should correspond to those techniques used in aging your face. For aging the hands with highlight and shadow, see Chapter 8; for aging the hands with liquid latex, see Chapter 10.

If you plan on using this makeup for film and television, more time and care must be taken. Be sure that all sections overlap the others and that no lumps or defects mar your application. Special attention must be paid to details around the eyes, hairline, and mouth. You cannot go over the latex with makeup; this will only nullify all your fine aging underneath.

Remember that makeup by itself is not the answer to any characterization. You must consider that the hairstyle, costume, and total physical adaptability are part of the whole aging process.

13

Three-Dimensional Makeup

This is a highly specialized and technically complex area of makeup requiring special materials, a good sized and well equipped lab, and, above all, some knowledge of art and sculpture. It is difficult to change a face from young to old, or to create a perfect likeness (an actor made-up to look exactly like someone else).

Extensive pre-production planning is necessary, which means weeks of preparation and hours of application. This is not only time-consuming but expensive, especially because these prosthetic pieces cannot be used more than once.

Claire Bloom as Queen Ann.

Marian Seldes as Henrieta Szeld.

Tom McDermott as George Bernard Shaw.

Prosthetics (foam latex) originally come in liquid form. Depending upon the manufacturer's formula, there are usually four basic ingredients: foam latex, curing paste, foaming agent, and gelling agent. Another formula includes: base latex, sulfur, zinc oxide, and gelling agent. Still another has three ingredients: latex, curing, and gelling. These ingredients, plus distilled water and colors, are measured precisely, stirred until they foam, poured into a mold, and placed in the oven to cure under controlled temperatures and timing. The result is a piece of foam rubber in the shape of a nose, a chin, or an entire face.

Mike Galloway as an old man.

1–3.

A full foam latex face, in spite of its size and thickness in certain areas, is very light and mobile. Every inch is glued to the actor's own face and moves with it. It is colored and textured to look like real skin, and if it is prepared and applied well no one can tell if it is an old man or young actor behind an old man's mask. The half-and-half photo shows the extent of the transformation.

4–5.

There is a vast difference between foam latex and regular latex. Examine these two cross-sections and you'll see. The photo on the left shows the foam latex face. It is spongy and thick, and it conforms perfectly to the actor's face because it has been made over an impression of his life mask. This allows free movement and expression inside as well as outside. The photo on the right shows the same mask made with liquid latex alone. It may be glued to the face only where the actor's profile coincides with the mask. The rest of the mask never touches the skin. Consequently, this kind of mask cannot move with the actor's face. It is suitable only for a single feature—a nose or a chin—and even then it should be used only in the theatre. Noses and chins for film and television must be made of foam latex.

1

2

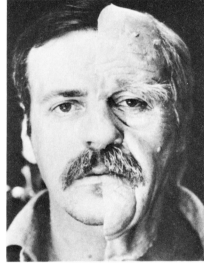

3

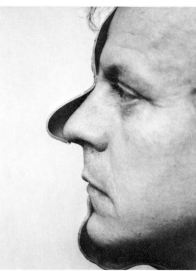

4

5

PART TWO

14

Stubble Beards

MATERIALS

1. Different shades of crepe hair, natural or synthetic fibers
2. Comb or brush
3. Scissors
4. Stubble beard adhesive
5. Foam rubber sponge
6. Eyebrow brush or toothbrush

APPLICATION

1.

When chopped, crepe hair (left) looks lumpy while natural or synthetic fibers (right) are clean, separate, and easier to use. However, you can use crepe hair if natural or synthetic fibers are unavailable.

2–3.

After selecting a color, comb or brush the hair to get out the kinks. Hold the hair between your fingers and cut it over a piece of cloth or table about $1/16''$ or shorter in length.

4.

Rub stubble beard adhesive over the beard and mustache area, smoothing it with your fingers and making sure you cover the entire area.

5.

Take a piece of foam rubber sponge and press it firmly over the chopped hairs.

1

2

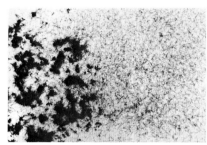

3

4

5

6

7

8

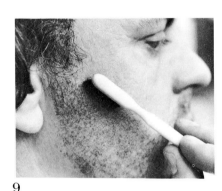

9

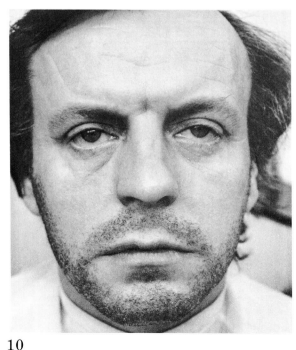

10

6.

Gently press the sponge over the wax base on your face.

7–8.

Continue until your entire face is covered. You might find a few lumpy areas here and there, especially if you're using chopped crepe hair. If this happens, take an eyebrow brush or toothbrush and very gently brush it off.

9.

While you have the brush in your hand, smooth and thin out the edges, getting rid of any hard lines.

10.

The result is a very natural stubble beard that won't come off unless you rub or scratch your face. To remove it, simply dampen a towel and rub off the beard and the (wax) adhesive.

This makeup, using natural or synthetic fibers, can be used for film and television, providing the makeup artist is careful not to leave any lumps or empty areas behind. Mixed shades and uneven edges insure a natural looking beard. Don't be hasty. Cut the hairs as short as you can and apply them carefully.

In the absence of crepe hair, use natural or synthetic fibers, and for five o'clock shadow, use Bob Kelly's Beard Stubble Black. It is a waxy material in a flat ¼-ounce container. Apply it with a stipple sponge carefully and evenly. Clean with cold cream or wash with soap and water.

15

Quick Beards and Mustaches with Crepe Hair

This technique, if followed carefully, is minimal in both cost and time—only a few cents for the material and ten or fifteen minutes for the application.

MATERIALS

1. Crepe hair, the color of the character's
2. Comb
3. Scissors
4. Spirit gum
5. Alcohol

APPLICATION

1.
Remove the cord from the braided hair.

2–3.
Take out all the kinks by spreading the hair apart with your fingers. Or, placing the piece on your knee, comb through it carefully.

4–5.
Then, holding the flat end in one hand and the braided end in the other, pull gently. The hair will separate.

1

2

3

4

5

6

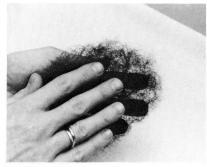

7

8

9

10

11

12

13

14

6.

Take the separated section and, if it is very thick, thin it by removing some of the hairs.

7.

Placing the remaining section in the palms of your hands, rub it back and forth, forming it to the general shape of the beard.

8.

Cut two triangular sections out of the top of the hairpiece, as shown, and discard them.

9.

Pull out two small pieces from the remaining crepe hair, as in step 5. Roll each one in the palms of your hands to be used as mustaches.

10.

Apply spirit gum on your chin and under it, down to your Adam's apple. Wait until it is very gummy (you can test it with the tip of your finger).

11.

Place the beard's three points at the center and corners of the lower lip. Then, with the help of your comb, push the top and bottom layers of hair against the skin, keeping the edges very thin and totally glued.

12.

Take the hanging section and tuck it gently under the chin, pressing to hold.

13.

The result—a chin beard.

14.

Apply spirit gum to the upper lip, place the mustache, and press to hold.

15–16.

Trim the entire chin beard and mustache gently with a scissors.

17–19.

If both sides of the face must be covered for a full beard, repeat step 5, pulling out two pieces for the sides. Apply spirit gum from the sideburn to the edge of the chin beard. When this is gummy, lay on the piece and blend it to the chin, keeping the edges thin by trimming. Do the same on the other side. Remember, this beard should not be thick. The thinner you make it, the better it will look.

Removal is accomplished simply by pulling off the hair and wiping the spirit gum off with alcohol.

It is best to use a ready-made beard and mustache for television and film. But, if necessary, this technique can be used for extras. It should not be used for leading characters or those subject to close-ups.

15

16

17

18

19

16

Laying on Beards and Mustaches with Crepe Hair

After you've decided what kind, shape, size, and color of beard your character needs, you must select the hair—either crepe or natural, straight or curly. In most cases, beards and mustaches are not only lighter than the hair on your head, but coarser, straighter, or curlier. They also contain different mixtures of shades. To mix colors, either comb them together in small bunches or apply different shades side by side. These can be worked with later to achieve a uniform mixture.

Let's say you're using curly crepe hair. You will need:

MATERIALS

1. Crepe hair of various shades
2. Comb
3. Spirit gum
4. Scissors
5. Silk cloth
6. Alcohol
7. Translucent powder
8. Hairspray

PREPARING CREPE HAIR

1.
Take the cord out of the braided hair.

1

2

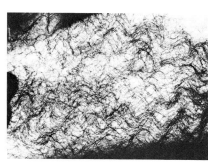

3

4

5

6

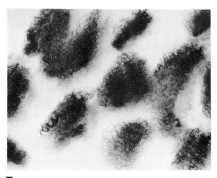

7

2–3.
Open the hair with your fingers. Then, placing it either on your lap or on a table, use a comb to open up all the curls, keeping in mind that the fibers should all go in one direction. Don't actually comb it through, except for the very end; just make it very kinky and open.

4.
To be sure all the curls and lumps have been removed, hold the hair against the light.

5–6.
Holding this piece in one hand, pull section by section from it.

7.
Place the sections on the table.

APPLICATION

Before gluing on the hair, look at figures 8 to 10. Figures 8 and 9 indicate the direction of the hair on the chin area, depending on the style of the beard; figure 10 shows how to glue on each bunch of crepe hair. This method must be followed or the beard will not be good-looking and natural.

11.

Apply spirit gum under and near the tip of your chin. Make sure it is gummy by tapping it with your finger.

12.

Pick up a thin bunch of hair; trim the ends of it with scissors.

13.

Place the hair over the spirit gum and press it with scissors, fingers, or a silk cloth. (If your fingers and scissors get sticky, which they will, clean them with alcohol or dip your fingers in powder.)

14.

If you follow the design, you'll have rows of crepe hair overlapping each other. (Don't leave wide gaps between the pieces. They should be glued side by side.)

15.

Following the process shown in figure 10, begin from the chin and move up toward the sideburn, pointing each bunch of hair in the direction that hair would grow naturally. The closer you get to the edge of the beard, the lighter the hairs will be and the less you'll have to glue. At the top of the cheeks you'll be able to see skin through the hairs.

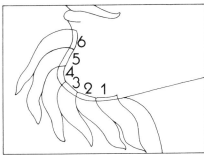

8

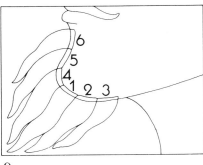
9

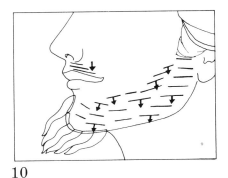
10

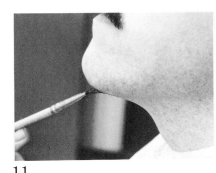
11

12

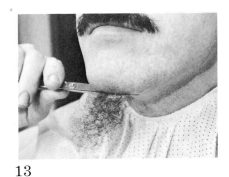
13

14

15

16

17

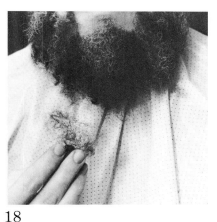

18

19

20

21

16.
When finished, you'll have unruly, messy hair on your face.

17.
A period of waiting is necessary for the spirit gum to dry. Meanwhile, take the silk cloth and press down the hairs to make sure they're all glued on. You can dampen the cloth with water.

18–19.
For thinning the beard either with your hand or a comb, very gently pull out some of the hairs. Although many of the unglued hairs will fall out, don't panic. What remains on your face will be sufficient for a nice beard.

20–21.
Don't use the scissors horizontally when cutting down your beard. If you cut it too short it will be impossible to fix. Instead, hold the scissors vertically and shape gently until you're satisfied.

22.

Holding your face in your hand, push the beard in place.

23.

Last minute adjustments—such as mixing and/or placing the light colored hairs in place, or opening a lumpy area—should be done with the end of a rattail comb.

24–25.

Hold a piece of paper over your eyes and spray the beard (or better, have someone do it for you).

26.

The end result should be a nice, full, curly beard. This, however, cannot be saved for another performance. To remove it, simply pull the hairs off and clean your face with alcohol or make-up remover.

22

23

24

25

26

27

28

29

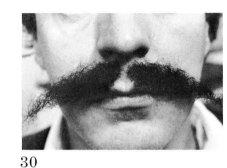

30

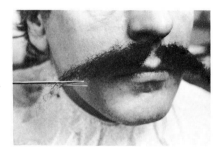

31

27–30.
Adding a mustache in layers (like the beard) with curly crepe hair is not any easy job. Take a bunch of the crepe hair you've already prepared and roll it in the palm of your hand. When it's ready, trim the tip and glue one piece on each side of the upper lip, leaving a narrow separation between the two pieces.

31–32.
Gently trim the mustache to the shape and length desired.

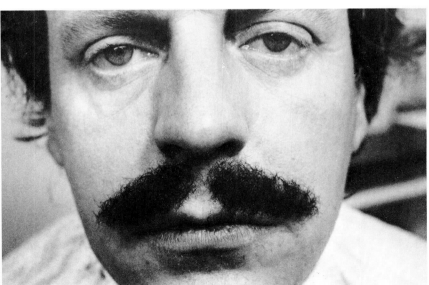

32

MATERIALS

For a short, straight beard, use the materials listed at the beginning of this chapter, but use straight crepe hair instead of curly.

1.

To straighten braided hair, take out the cords and submerge the hair in hot water. After removing it, squeeze out the water and hang it up overnight. This method will retain some of the natural wave, if needed in the long braid. If straight hair is required in a hurry, place it over an ironing board and press to dry.

2.

Cut the colors you have selected to the beard's exact length and line them up in front of you.

3.

All the application techniques explained in this chapter apply here, with one exception; after you have applied the spirit gum, pick up each bunch of hair, take out a small section, and press it over the spirit gum. Make sure the area is tacky.

4–5.

Proceed with the hair under the chin area.

6.

Add the light and dark shades of crepe hair over the chin, unless a solid color is desired.

1

2

3

4

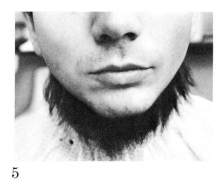

5

6

7-8.
With a mixture of both shades, light and dark, extend the beard all the way to the sideburns. Keep it even and thin.

9.
Apply the mustache in the same way.

10.
Keep the top edges light and thin by laying on a few hairs at a time.

11.
When finished, wait until the hairs are completely dry and then—as explained previously in steps 18 to 25 of this chapter—comb, trim, and spray to hold.

Both of these techniques should be used in television and film only when ready-made beards and mustaches cannot be obtained. Extreme care must be taken when mixing the hairs, so that the edges are clean, thin, and natural looking. Use matte spirit gum as an adhesive; or, tap the regular spirit gum with the tip of your finger—this will make it gummy as well as matte.

7

8

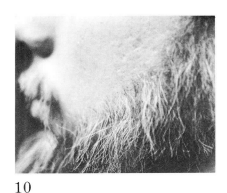

9

10

11

Application of Ready-Made Beards and Mustaches

MATERIALS

1. Ready-made beard and mustache
2. Spirit gum
3. Scissors
4. Silk cloth

For ordering the correct size, shape, and style of beard and mustache you will need:

1. Plastic sheet or Saran Wrap
2. Roll of Scotch tape
3. Eyebrow pencil

APPLICATION

1.
Wrap the lower part of your face with plastic or Saran Wrap.

2–3.
If no one can help cover and secure the shape of it with Scotch tape, hold the plastic sheet on your head with masking tape. A piece of tissue beneath the tape will prevent it from sticking to your hair.

4–5.
Outline the beard and mustache area with an eyebrow pencil. On each side, mark where the sideburn ends and two inches higher.

3

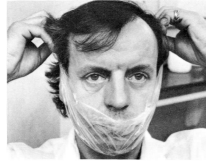

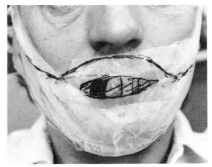

1

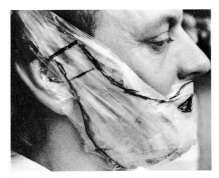

2

5

6

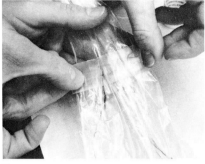

7

8

9

10

11

12

6–7.
Cover the entire marking with tape.

8.
Remove and add a few sections of tape inside to hold the plastic sheet in shape. Specify the color, style, size, and shape of the beard and send it to Bob Kelly* several weeks before the performance.

9–10.
You will receive a full beard and mustache just as ordered. Since it is made with fine lace, you must be careful in handling and applying it.

11–12.
Hold the beard against your face, and if necessary, cut off about an inch or so from each sideburn, leaving one inch to be glued under your own hair. Use only a razor blade and cut the lace from the back.

*Check with the appropriate UK stockist.

13.
Apply spirit gum on and under your chin, as far as the lace extends.

14.
When gummy, place the center of the beard on your chin and press to hold; tuck in the section underneath and press to hold.

15.
Apply spirit gum to the side of your face (one side at a time) only where the beard will be placed. Lay on the beard and press. Opening your mouth slightly will create enough "give" to make your speaking or laughing easier.

16–17.
Using a rattail comb or pencil, make a separation where the beard overlaps your sideburn. Holding up your hair, apply spirit gum to this area.

18.
Lay on the beard and drape your own hair over it, creating a continuous line between your hair and the beard.

19–20.
A mustache comes in one piece. You can glue it on as a whole and then, when secure, split the center of it with a scissors. Again, this will give you more ease in speaking, laughing, or singing.

Providing that the original order was correct, you will have the right beard. If you try it on and feel you must change the shape, trim while you're wearing it.

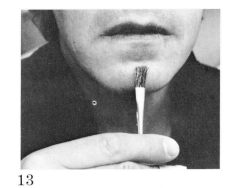
13

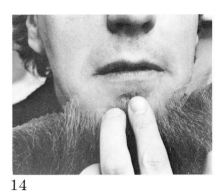
14

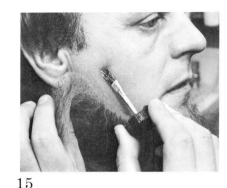
15

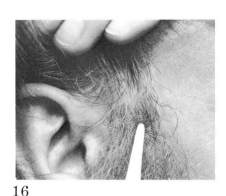
16

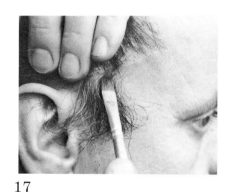
17

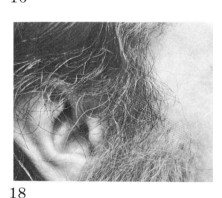
18

19

20

21.

Holding your scissors vertically, cut and trim very gently as you go until the beard is the right length for your character.

If you have to open your mouth for more than talking and laughing (if, for instance, you have to sing), it would be best to use one of the other techniques discussed earlier. Or, if you must use ready-made beards for continuity, you will have to cut it in at least five sections—two sections for each side and one for the chin, as shown in the drawing.

22.

To cut a lace beard, use a razor blade and very gently split the lace—not the hair—from the back (see the dotted lines in the drawing). To glue these sections, begin with the chin first. Section two is second, and then section three. Place them as close to each other as you can. This will give you the easy movement of the facial muscles you need for singing.

23.

The final result.

Gently remove the beard and clean the lace inside. This is done by placing the lace over a paper towel and, using a toothbrush dipped in alcohol, dissolving the spirit gum onto the towel.

Ready-made beards and mustaches are ideal for television and film. Since the lace will

21

22

23

be seen in close-ups in both media (especially film), you or the makeup artist in charge should cut it as close to the hair as possible. After gluing it down with matte spirit gum, cover the lace with layers of hair glued to the skin (see Chapter 18, steps 41–46) for a natural look.

18

The Construction and Application of Beards and Mustaches Made on Latex

MATERIALS

1. Different shades of crepe hair, natural or synthetic fibers
2. Comb
3. Wooden or plaster beard block
4. Japanese or regular ⅜" brush
5. Cup of water
6. Cake of soap
7. Paper towels
8. Liquid latex
9. Hand hair dryer
10. Spatula
11. Regular and thinning scissors
12. Hair brush
13. Curling irons and stove
14. Translucent powder
15. Spirit gum
16. Alcohol or acetone

After you've determined the shape, length, color, and period of the beard and mustache for your character, choose the appropriate hair and you're ready to begin.

APPLICATION

1–2.
If you're using crepe hair, open it up and take out the cords.

1

2

3

4

5

3.
If you want a curly beard, just brush or comb the crepe hair.

4.
If you want a straight or slightly wavy beard, dip the crepe hair into hot water and hang it up to dry overnight. Or, if you're in a hurry, press it over an ironing board.

5.
Holding the crepe hair in one hand, pull out sections with the other.

6.
Place the sections next to you, using enough for a full beard and mustache. Make sure you have some light hairs handy to mix or add here and there, especially at the very edges.

7.
If you are using natural or synthetic fibers, as pictured here, comb and cut the sizes you want—an inch or so longer than the final length of the beard, as a rule, which should allow enough for cutting and curling.

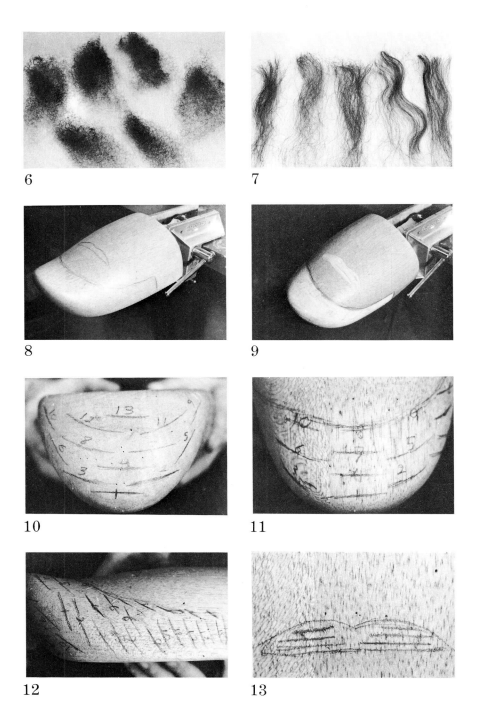

6

7

8

9

10

11

12

13

8.

Secure the beard block to the edge of a work table, and mark the outline of the beard and mustache.

9.

Dip the Japanese brush (or regular ⅜″ brush) in water, rub it over a cake of soap, and press it over a paper towel to soak up the excess water. Then dip the brush in the liquid latex and cover the area you have outlined on the beard block. Dry with a hand hair dryer and repeat the process until you have about six or seven layers. Keep the edges very thin.

Clean your brush after each layer by rinsing it in clear water, rubbing it over the soap, and pressing it over the paper towel. It is now ready for the next layer.

Pictures 10 through 13 show how to lay beards and mustaches on the block.

10.

This represents the area under the chin, beginning with the top and going row by row towards the neck.

11.

This is the front of the chin, beginning with the tip and extending towards the lower lip.

12.

Pictured here is the method of laying beards from the lower part of the jaw and the side of the face towards the sideburns.

13.

For the mustache, extend only three or four thin layers towards the nose on each side, leaving the center very thin.

14–15.

When trimming hairs for the mustache, cut them at angles and lay them in a straight line so the mustache extends to the sides rather than down (unless the latter effect is desired).

16–17.

Turn the beard block over and, beginning under the chin, apply a section of liquid latex ½″ × 2″. Adhere the hairs you have selected by pressing them with your fingers or a spatula until they are soaked in latex. Repeat, covering the entire area of the beard and mustache with rows of small, overlapping sections. It will take a long time. Keep each section of hair as thin and close to the last row as possible (except at the very edges), using a mixture of dark and light shades.

18–19.

The result will be a very bushy, untidy beard and mustache. Allow it to dry overnight.

14

15

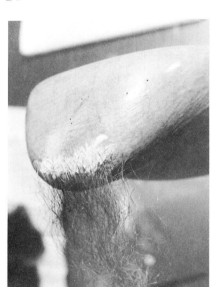

16

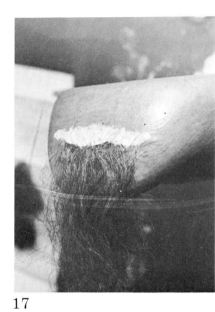

17

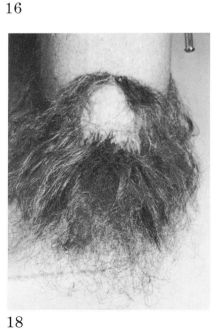

18

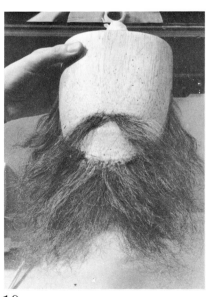

19

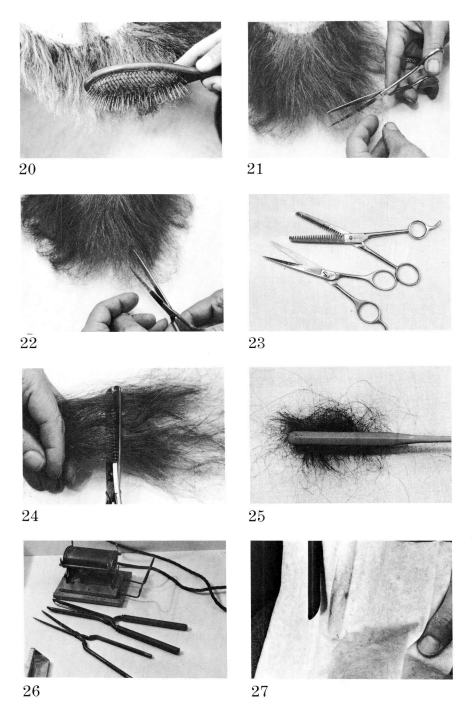

20

21

22

23

24

25

26

27

20.

The next day, while the beard is still on the block, brush out the loose hairs or pull them out with your fingers. Be careful not to pull out too many.

21.

Do not hold your scissors horizontally when cutting the beard to the proper length or you might cut it too short. If you do, the chances of fixing it are very slim.

22.

Holding the scissors vertically, trim and cut gently as you go along.

23.

If you wish to thin the beard, you'll need special thinning shears with lots of "teeth."

24–25.

Holding the hairs at the root or tip of the beard, make one firm cut. Be extremely careful while using thinning shears, as only one cut can remove a lot of hair.

26.

If the beard needs curling, you'll need two sizes of curling irons: a thin one for the mustache and a thick one for the beard. You'll also need a stove to heat the irons.

27.

Before curling the beard, make sure the irons are not hot enough to burn. Test by curling a piece of the discarded hair or by pressing it on a piece of Kleenex. If the hair or the Kleenex burns, let the irons cool off.

28.

Holding the hair gently between the blades, curl under or up, whichever is desired. Pressing too hard could cause a ridge to form on the hair.

29.

After the mustache is cut to the desired length, take the thin iron and place the blade under the hairs, lifting and curling gently. *Do not* press hard.

This cutting, trimming, and curling is done with the beard and mustache on the beard block. There is no adequate way to explain the procedure; it simply requires practice, and probably burning a few pieces, before getting it right.

30.

The final result.

31–32.

To lift the beard off the block, first loosen one sideburn. Then, using a brush dipped in powder, gently pull off the latex.

When applying the beard, place it on your face and hold it from sideburn to sideburn. If you've measured correctly, this new piece should extend about an inch or so over your own sideburns. Don't cut anything at this time.

28

30

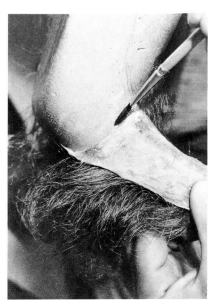

31

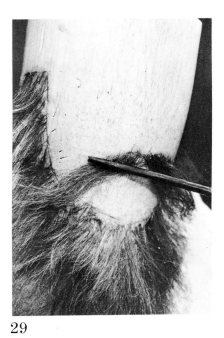

29

32

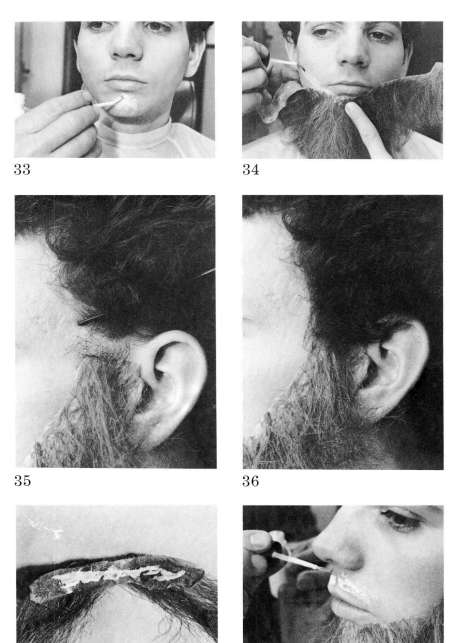

33

34

35

36

37

38

33.
Begin by applying liquid latex, not spirit gum, over and under the chin area only.

34.
Apply the beard over the latex, making sure it's correctly placed, and hold. Then apply liquid latex to one side of the face, place the beard, and hold again. Do the same for the other side.

35.
To match the beard with your own hair, lay about ¼″ of the beard over your sideburns and cut the rest. Then, lifting each sideburn with the end of a rat-tail comb or a pencil, press the beard against your skin.

36.
Drape your sideburns over the beard. For a better hold, glue down the beard by applying latex to the face and spirit gum to the sideburn area. (Spirit gum is easier to remove.) If the color of your hair does not match the color of your beard, you can try to darken the latex beard at the sideburns or lighten your own hair.

37–38.
Liquid latex can be applied at the back of the mustache or on your upper lip before placing the mustache.

39.

After you've applied your foundation, you'll discover that the color of the latex beard is different—especially at the edges where it's very thin. Take a brush and apply some makeup over the latex to match the foundation.

39

40.

The front looks good.

40

41.

On the sides you'll find a very sharp edge where the latex beard ends. To get rid of this, apply touches of spirit gum—about ¼″—on your skin near the latex piece.

41

42.

Select several light shades of hairs, lay them gently on your skin, and press down with scissors or a silk cloth. Do the same for the top of the mustache.

42

43.

Another way of doing this is to dip the ends of the hairs in spirit gum and press them on gently.

43

44–45.

The end result will be a natural looking beard and mustache.

44

46.

To remove, gently loosen one end and separate it from your skin, leaving only the hairs that you've added to cover the edges. (This beard, by the way, is very flexible and stretches unlike any other type. When you're wearing it you can move your facial muscles in any direction; you can even sing with it.) After cleaning the back of the beard,

45

46

place it on the block so it's ready to use again. Clean the added hair and spirit gum with alcohol or acetone.

Remember that this technique is designed for the theatre, where the same style of beard is needed every night and where it's not practical economically for the company to buy or rent a ready-made one. It should only be used for television and film in emergencies—and only if it's carefully made, making sure the latex edges are well covered.

If a beard block is not available you can apply this beard directly to your face or, better still, to a plaster impression of your face made as follows.

For this procedure you will need someone to help you.

MATERIALS

1. Vaseline
2. One roll of 2″ plaster bandage
3. One roll of 4″ plaster bandage
4. Bowl of warm water
5. Scissors
6. Spatula
7. Plaster of Paris
8. File
9. Sandpaper
10. Clear shellac

Before beginning the impression, cover yourself with a towel or makeup cape.

APPLICATION

1.

Apply a generous amount of Vaseline to your sideburns as well as two inches above. Then cover your entire face and chin.

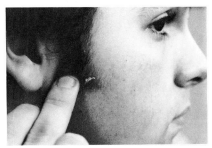

1

3

2–3.

Cut the 4″ plaster bandage in sections long enough to cover your face from one sideburn to the other.

4.

Saturate one piece at a time with warm water.

5.

Squeeze out the water, open the piece, and place the center of the strip under your chin and the two ends over your sideburns. Hold it there while your helper presses it to take the shape of your face. Repeat this process a few times so your chin is covered as far as your beard grows.

6.

Apply a few layers as far as possible across your mouth, chin, and upper lip and mustache areas, continuing until you've finished the 4″ roll. Make sure you have even layers and even thickness all around.

2

4

5

6

7.

Cut the 2″ roll in sections long enough to pass over your nose, and lay the two ends on either side of your face. Repeat this until you have good coverage. (Save about a foot of the 2″ bandage for later use.) Leave the tip of your nose free for breathing.

8.

After the plaster bandage is dry, move your facial muscles underneath and then remove it. If some of your hairs pull, gently separate them with a spatula.

9–10.

Now fold the extra piece of bandage you've set aside. Saturate it in water, squeeze it out, and cover the open tip of your nose from the outside. Let it dry. This is the negative of the lower part of your face.

11.

To make the "positive," apply a generous layer of Vaseline inside the "negative."

12.

Mix plaster of Paris in warm water—thick enough so it's not runny—and fill up the inside of the piece, about an inch all over.

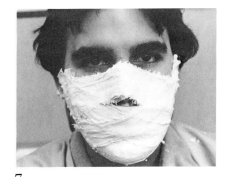
7

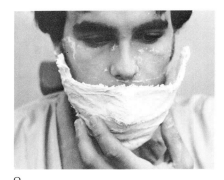
8

9

10

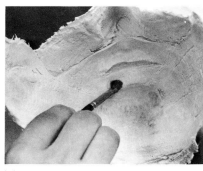
11

12

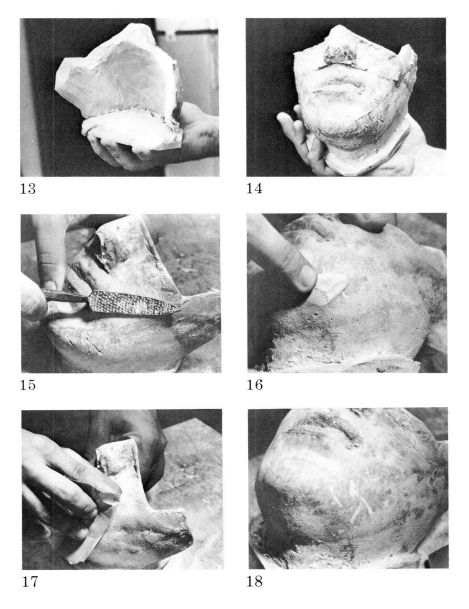

13
14
15
16
17
18

13.
Add a plaster base so it can stand by itself.

14.
When totally dry, remove the plaster bandage.

15.
Use a file to get rid of the rough areas.

16.
Fill any holes or defects in the impression by mixing some plaster in a small cup and rubbing it all over the mask. Let it dry.

17.
Smooth the entire mask with sandpaper, brush off the powdered plaster, and spray or brush on several coats of clear shellac.

18.
It's ready to be used.

19

Mutton Chops and Sideburns

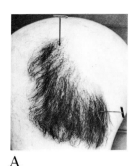

A

B

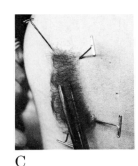

C

Photographs A and B are a mutton chop and a sideburn respectively (they come in pairs). If you don't already have mutton chops or long sideburns on your face—and you have to have one or the other for the character you are portraying—you can order what you need ahead of time and apply them like a regular lace beard.

Ready-made Mutton Chops or Sideburns

MATERIALS

1. Pair of mutton chops or sideburns
2. Spirit gum
3. Silk cloth
4. Comb
5. Eyebrow pencil, the color of your hair

If the mutton chops or sideburns you've ordered need more curl to match your hair (or if you have an old pair of mutton chops or sideburns without any curls), the best way of curling them is to pin them on a cloth or Styrofoam wig block (C), and curl them with a mustache curling iron.

APPLICATION

1.

Apply spirit gum in the area

2

1

3

4

where you'll be attaching the piece.

2.

When tacky, place the piece over the gum high enough so it overlaps your own sideburns by about half an inch.

3.

Using a rattail comb or the end of the spirit gum brush, make a separation where the piece overlaps your sideburn; hold the hair up and apply spirit gum to the part.

4.

Place the lace over the gummy part; press with a silk cloth to hold, combing your own hair over the mutton chop or sideburn to create a continuous line. If your hair at the temples and sideburns is thinner than the added piece, fill in these areas with eyebrow pencil. (See Chapter 1 on corrective makeup.)

Mutton Chops
and Sideburns
with Crepe Hair

MATERIALS

1. Crepe hair the color of your hair or a shade or two lighter
2. Comb
3. Scissors
4. Spirit gum
5. Hair spray

APPLICATION

1.

Remove the cord from the braided hair.

2.

Take out all the kinks by spreading the hair apart with your fingers. Or, placing the piece on your knee, comb through it carefully, making sure you don't lose any of the hairs.

3.

Then, holding the flat end in one hand and the braided end in the other, pull gently. The hair will separate.

4.

If you divide this piece into two sections, you'll have a pair of mutton chops or sideburns.

5.

Place each section in the palm of your hand and rub it back and forth.

6.

Cut each one to the desired size.

1

2

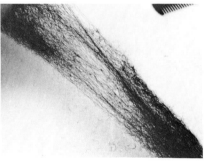

3

4

5

6

7.

Apply spirit gum to the area where the new piece will go. When tacky, place and press it down to hold. Do the same with the other side, combing in your own hair to create a continuous line.

8.

Trim and spray to hold.

9.

The end result.

10.

If you need a mustache, attach it to the mutton chops. Pull out a thin section from the crepe hair, roll it in the palm of your hand, and cut it to size.

11.

Apply spirit gum to the area, attach the mustache piece, and connect it to the mutton chops for a perfect facial hairpiece.

7

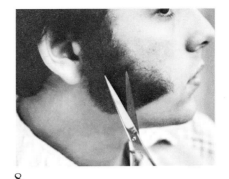
8

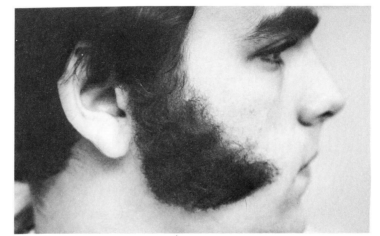
9

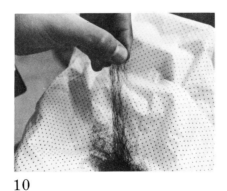
10

11

Mutton Chops or Sideburns with Very Short Crepe, Natural, or Synthetic Fibers

MATERIALS

1. Crepe, natural, or synthetic fibers
2. Scissors
3. Spirit gum

If you are using crepe hair, remove the cords and submerge the hair in hot water. Then squeeze it out and hang it up to dry overnight. If you need it in a hurry, place it over an ironing board and press to dry.

APPLICATION

1.
Cut the hair to the desired length.

2.
Apply spirit gum to the area, one section at a time (in this case we're laying on mutton chops and a mustache).

3.
Pick up a bunch of hairs and pull out a small section.

4–5.
Place this section over the gum, applying it from the center of the upper lip to the bottom of the mutton chops and then upwards toward the sideburns. Keep the sections close together, light, and thin, especially at the edges. Make sure there is no line of demarcation between this application and your sideburns.

6.
Wait until dry, then trim and cut.

7.
The final result.

Mutton chops and sideburns of natural or synthetic fibers are suitable for film and television. Crepe hair is not realistic enough, and should be used only on the stage.

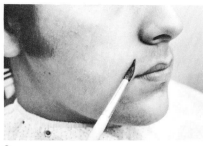

1

2

3

4

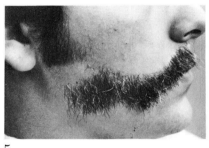

5

6

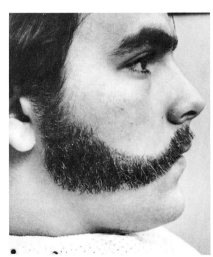

7

20

Application of Wigs and Falls

Ordering a Wig

If you're going to have a wig made for you, be sure to contact the wigmaker several weeks before the production. Here is the way to send your order. (For this procedure you'll need someone to help you.)

MATERIALS

1. One sheet of clear plastic
2. A roll of clear Scotch tape
3. Eyebrow pencil, black or brown

PROCESS OF TAKING THE PATTERN

1.
Place the plastic sheet or Saran Wrap over your head, twist the sides, and hold it tight.

2–3.
Cover the plastic sheet with a layer of Scotch tape to hold the shape.

4.
Trace your entire hairline with an eyebrow pencil.

5.
To avoid smearing the pencil marks, cover them with a layer of Scotch tape.

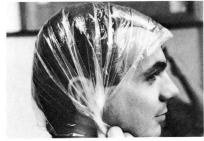

1

2

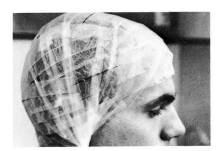

3

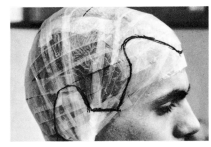

4

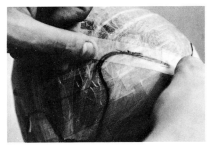

5

6

7

6–7.
Take off the cap and place a few strips of Scotch tape inside, so it holds together. To this pattern attach a sample of the necessary hair color, mentioning the period of the play and the character you are portraying. If possible, include a picture of the period or style of wig desired.

Fitting Wigs
on Men

MATERIALS

1. Wig
2. Scissors and pinking shears
3. Matte spirit gum
4. Silk cloth
5. Bobby pins
6. Comb, brush, and hair spray

All wigs, as a rule, have lace fronts. The lace on wigs used in film and television, however, is much finer than that used in the theatre.

There are two different methods of attaching wigs, based on the type of role the actor will be playing.

APPLICATION FOR VIOLENT (OR FAST-MOVING) SCENES

1.
Spray and comb the hair as flat as possible.

2–3.
Put up your hair in pincurls (mostly in back of the head) using bobby pins, keeping the front as flat as possible.

4–5.
Put on the wig, attaching it to the pincurls at various strategic points with bobby pins or hair pins. Make sure your own hair is totally covered. If the lace in front is wider than ¾", cut it with a scissors, preferably pinking shears.

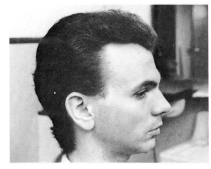

1

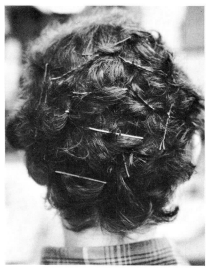

2

3

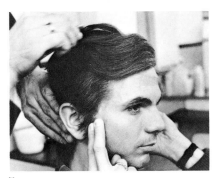

4

5

6.
Gently lifting up the front, apply matte spirit gum under the lace.

7.
Place the lace over the gum and press down with a damp silk cloth until the lace adheres to the skin.

8.
Repeat the previous step on both sides, making sure the wig covers your own hair.

9.
Comb, dress, and spray to hold.

6

7

8

APPLICATION FOR NON-VIOLENT SCENES (NO STRONG WIND, NO WILD DANCE NUMBERS, ETC.)

1.
Spray and comb the hair as flat as possible.

2–3.
Omit the pincurls—they're not necessary.

4.
Put on the wig, making sure your own hair is covered. If the lace in front is wider than ¾″, cut it with a scissors, preferably pinking shears.

5–9.
Follow the gluing procedure outlined in steps 6 to 9 above.

9

Fitting Wigs on Women

LONG HAIR

If you have long hair and need a period hairdo, the addition of different pieces—such as switches, falls, or clusters—can be more economical than using a complete wig. It's also easier to create different styles this way (see photos A–F on page 113).

If you're wearing a wig, perhaps a short one, and it's not the same color as your own hair:

1–3.
Make a few pincurls on the top and sides of your head.

4.
Twist your own hair—as in a French twist—and pin it up tight and neat.

5–6.
Put on the wig. If there's a small comb sewn inside, push it under the pincurl nearest your forehead and pull down the wig.

7.
Pin the wig to the pincurls, making sure it's tight and secure.

8–9.
Dress, comb, and spray.

Make sure your own hair doesn't show underneath. A soft hair style on your forehead and around your face will help cover your hair line.

1

2

3

4

5

7

6

8

9

SHORT HAIR

The addition of stock pieces can be a help if you have short hair (depending on the period and how good your hairdresser is), but if you have to wear a wig, particularly one darker than your own hair:

1–3.
Place three pincurls on the top of your head, two on each side (temples and above the ears) and two at the back.

4–5.
Put on the wig, pin it to the pincurls, and then dress, comb, and spray it. Make sure your own hair line doesn't show.

6–8.
These photos show what you can do with the same wig. Putting it on back to front will make it appear longer; this will also give a nice tousled, windblown look, if required. (Only machine-made stretch wigs can do this.)

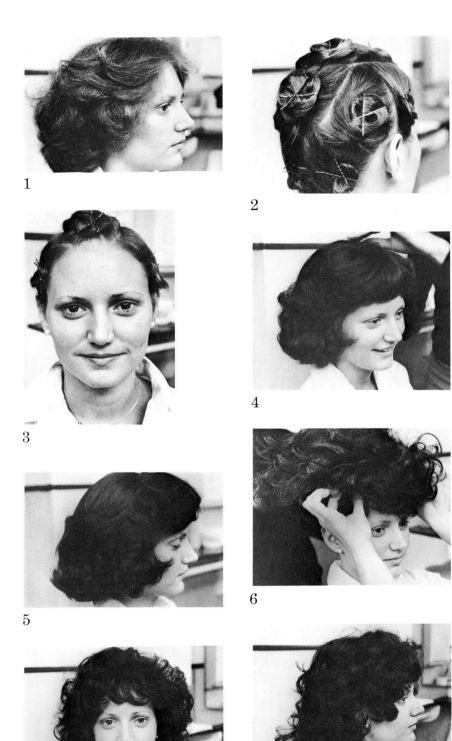

1

2

3

4

5

6

7

8

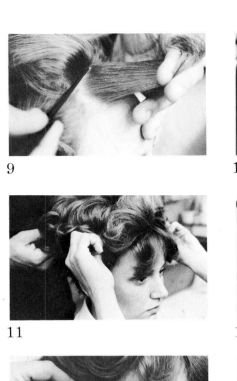

9

10

11

12

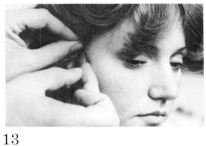

13

14

15

16

17

If you're wearing a wig that matches the color of your own hair, place two pincurls on top rather than three, two on each side, and two at the back of the head and neck line. Then:

9–10.
Open a part at the front of the head and comb the hair forward.

11–12.
Place the wig on the part.

13–14.
Pin the wig to each pincurl.

15–17.
Comb your own hair on top to match the wig's dressing, then spray to hold.

Falls

The fall, made for period shows, can be worn instead of a wig only if you have a fairly good head of hair.

MATERIALS

1. Fall
2. Bobby pins
3. Long hair clips
4. Comb, brush, and hair spray

APPLICATION

1.

Depending on the width of the fall, make a part in the back of the head from ear to ear. Comb the front section forward and hold it down with hair clips or bobby pins.

2.

Make half a dozen pincurls at the back of the head from side to side.

3–4.

Place the fall over the parted area and pin it to the pincurls all the way across.

5–6.

Take out the clips and comb your own hair over the fall. Dress and spray to hold.

If you have very short hair and are doing a period piece, you definitely need a wig. But an actor with long hair can use it to his advantage in period pieces by combing, dressing, and curling it. Men can apply sideburns or mutton chops as needed (see Chapter 19).

A = Model's own hair

B = Fall to be added

1

2

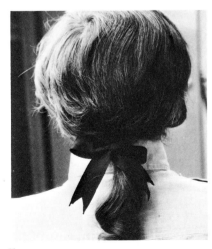

3

4

5

6

The accompanying photos illustrate the variety of hair styles that can be created with period or contemporary wigs. Observe how each can transform one face into many different "looks." (The face is Barbara Kelly's; the hairstylist is Werner Sherer.)

1940's

1940's

1930's

1960's

1920's

A

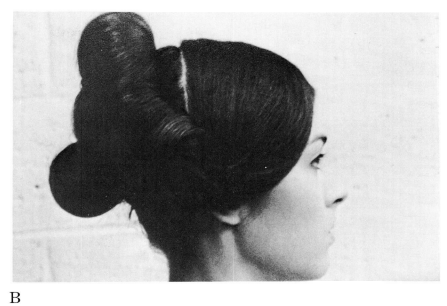

B

C

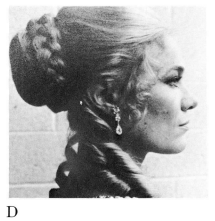

D

F

E

21

Constructing a Hairpiece

If you're bald on top and need a hairpiece to match your own hair or that of the character you're portraying, you can either buy or rent one (these must be ordered weeks in advance) or you can make an exact pattern of your bald spot and construct your own hairpiece.

MATERIALS

1. One sheet of clear plastic
2. A roll of clear Scotch tape
3. Eyebrow pencil, black or brown
4. Scissors
5. Head block made of plaster, wood, or Styrofoam
6. Liquid latex
7. Japanese brush or regular ⅜" brush
8. Hand hair dryer
9. Cake of soap
10. Cup of water
11. Paper towels
12. Crepe hair (curly or straight), natural hair or synthetic fibers
13. Spatula or butter knife
14. Comb and brush
15. Translucent powder and puff
16. Double masking tape or toupee tape
17. Alcohol

1

PROCESS OF TAKING THE PATTERN

1.
In this procedure you'll need someone to help you. Place the plastic sheet or Saran Wrap over your head, twist the sides, and hold it tight.

2–3.
Cover the entire plastic sheet with a layer of Scotch tape to hold the shape.

4.
Using an eyebrow pencil, trace the bald spot over the Scotch-taped plastic sheet.

5.
To avoid smearing, cover the pencil mark with a layer of Scotch tape.

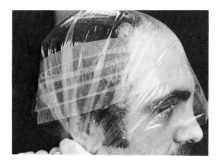

2

3

4

5

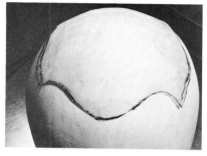

6

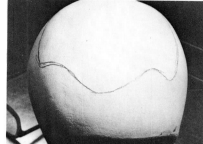

7

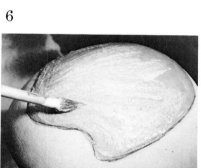

8

9

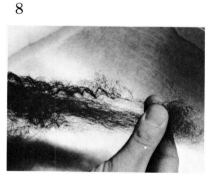

10

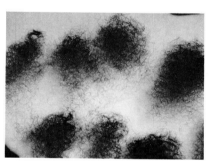

11

6.

Take off the cap, cut out the pattern, and place it on top of a head block.

7.

Using an eyebrow pencil, trace the outline of the pattern onto the head block. Remove the pattern and save it, in case your first attempt is not successful.

CONSTRUCTION OF THE HAIRPIECE

8.

Apply at least six or eight generous layers of liquid latex to the inside of the pattern, drying each layer before brushing on the next. (To save your brush, rinse it out with water after each layer, rub it over a cake of soap, and press it over a paper towel to soak up the excess water.)

9.

By now you've probably decided what type of hair to use. Let's assume you're using crepe hair and that it's supposed to be curly. Take out the cord and separate the curls with a comb or brush. For straight hair, dip the hair in hot water and hang it up to dry overnight. If you're in a hurry, press it over an ironing board.

10–11.

Take the combed strand in one hand and use the other to pull out the sections one by one, laying them on the table. Be sure these sections are not thick and unmanageable.

12.

Take one section at a time, place it at the edge of the table, and, using a spatula or butter knife, saturate about ¼″ of hair with latex.

13.

Lift and trim the uneven edge with scissors.

14.

Place the hair at the front edge of the pattern and press it down with scissors or a spatula, making sure it's glued before continuing.

15.

Keep in mind the exact pattern for laying the hair, which should resemble the one pictured here. Place and glue each section of the hair over these lines, working from the outside to the inside.

16–17.

Step by step, fill in the entire pattern with hair. When finished, leave it overnight to dry completely.

18.

On the following day, take the piece from the head block and attach a few strips of toupee tape or double masking tape to the back.

12

13

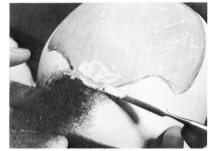

14

15

16

17

18

19.

Peel the paper off the tape.

20–22.

Clean your entire bald spot with alcohol to remove the natural oils. Then place the piece over your head, making sure it's in the right spot. Press to hold. Comb, brush, cut, and trim—or even thin it out, if you must, using thinning shears—to the desired length and shape.

19

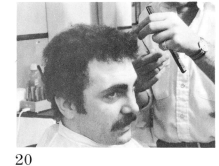

20

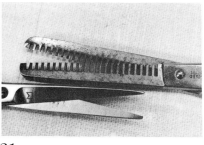

21

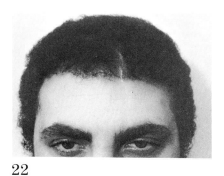

22

23-24.

"Before" and "after." The end result will not be satisfactory unless you begin with a clear idea about the color, texture, shape, and style of hair you want. Practice a few times before attempting the final construction, especially if you decide to use natural or synthetic fibers.

This technique is recommended for use in the theatre when the purchase of a hairpiece is not feasible. (It can only be used in television and film for actors not subject to close-ups.) The color must be a perfect match for the actor's own hair, and cutting or styling must be done by a professional hairstylist.

23

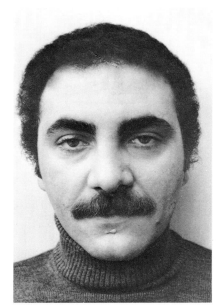

24

Nose and Chin

No part of the face changes a person's character and appearance more than his nose and chin, as you can see in the following photographs (A–H).

Constructing a Wax Nose

MATERIALS

1. Light brown eyebrow pencil
2. Spirit gum
3. Wax
4. Small spatula
5. Cup of water
6. Cold cream
7. ⅜″ brush
8. Sealer
9. Sponges (stipple or red rubber, foam rubber)
10. Rubber mask grease
11. Red-A Creme Stick
12. Translucent powder and puff
13. Alcohol

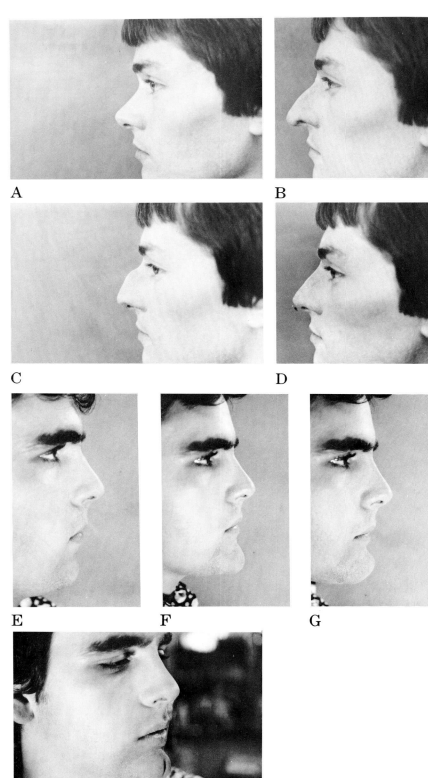

A

B

C

D

E

F

G

H

APPLICATION

Begin with an idea for the shape of the nose, making sure it's appropriate for the character you'll be portraying. Keep a sketch of it in front of you, if necessary.

1.

Using a light brown eyebrow pencil, mark the outline for the wax nose—that is, the area to which it will actually adhere on your own skin.

2.

Apply spirit gum inside the outline and wait until it becomes very gummy. You can speed this up or test it by tapping the spirit gum a few times with the tip of your finger.

3.

Place a small amount of wax over the spirit gum, press firmly, and spread to cover the gummy area. Now begin modeling. You can add more wax, if needed, as you go along. *Do not begin with a big amount of wax; it will only create more trouble.*

4.

Use your finger for modeling. (Or, if necessary, a spatula, butter knife, or any modeling tool can also be used.)

5.

When your fingers get sticky, as they will, dip them in water (do this as often as possible). After you've finished the modeling to your satisfaction, smooth it out by dipping the tip of your finger in cold cream (this should be used very sparingly).

1

2

3

4

5

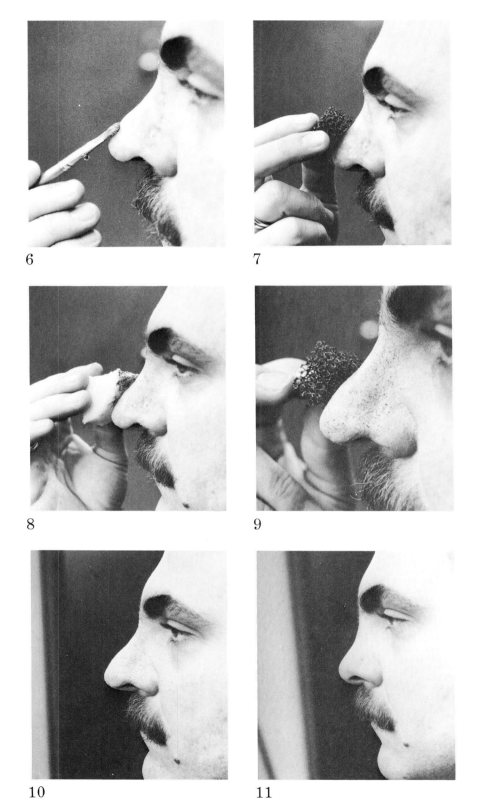

6

7

8

9

10

11

6.
Using a ⅜″ brush, apply several layers of sealer on top of the wax. Wait until it dries before proceeding.

7.
Create texture with a stipple sponge by pressing it gently over the sealed wax.

8.
Color with rubber mask grease, using a foam rubber sponge as an applicator, and blend into the foundation. The shades should be identical (mix several shades of rubber mask grease).

9.
If you find that the color of the wax nose needs further toning, use a stipple sponge or red rubber sponge to apply a gentle, sparing touch of Red-A Creme Stick. (Remember, you can always add more.) Apply the rest of your makeup and powder your entire face. Before leaving the makeup room, clean your sealer brush in acetone. Be sure to give yourself adequate time for this whole procedure, keeping in mind that a little practice goes a long way.

10–11.
"After" and "before," for comparison.

Constructing a Clay Nose

If the wax nose becomes an impossible task because of its stickiness, try working with a clay nose. While it won't stick to your fingers, your nose, or to a gummy area, it will stick to wax.

MATERIALS

1. Light brown eyebrow pencil
2. Spirit gum
3. Wax
4. Number 2 or 3 white clay, known as "Roma Plastilina" (since number 2 clay is softer and somewhat stickier than number 3, the latter is recommended)
5. Cup of water
6. Alcohol
7. Spatula or other modeling tool
8. ⅜" brush
9. Sealer
10. Acetone
11. Stipple or red rubber sponge
12. Rubber mask grease
13. Red-A Creme Stick
14. Translucent powder and puff

APPLICATION

Begin with a definite idea about the shape of the nose you have in mind for your character, or keep a sketch in front of you.

1.

Using a light brown eyebrow pencil, mark the outline for the clay nose—that is, the area it will actually adhere to on your own skin.

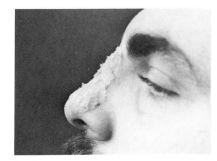

1–3.

2.

Apply spirit gum inside the outline and wait until it becomes very gummy. You can speed this up or test it by tapping the spirit gum a few times with the tip of your finger.

3.

Spread a very thin and uneven layer of wax over the gummy area.

4.

Take a small amount of clay, press it firmly over the wax, and begin your modeling. *Do not* use a large amount; you can always add to it as you go along. Dip your finger in cold water or alcohol when necessary.

5–6.

Any modeling tool can be used in addition to your finger for cutting, shaping, etc.

7.

When satisfied, cover the nose with several layers of sealer, using a ⅜" brush as an applicator. When you've finished, clean the brush in acetone.

4

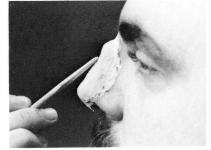

5

6

7

8

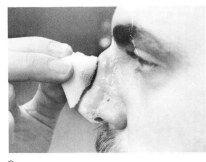

9

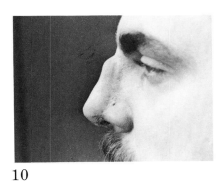

10

11

8.

Create texture with a stipple or red rubber sponge after the sealer is dry.

9.

Color with rubber mask grease and blend into the foundation.

You'll find that the color of the nose is a little different from the foundation. Stipple on some Red-A Creme Stick, very gently and sparingly, to get the right tone. Powder your entire face when you're totally finished.

10–11.

See the comparison.

Duplication of a Wax or Clay Nose in Latex

If you are performing for more than one night, the process described above can become tedious. Since there's no guarantee, furthermore, that you can duplicate the same shape and size again, the solution is to achieve a permanent duplication of the wax or clay nose in latex. For this process you will need:

MATERIALS

1. Vaseline
2. Two ⅜″ brushes (one for plaster and one for Vaseline)
3. A plastic bowl or paper cup
4. Plaster of Paris
5. Spatula or butter knife

PROCEDURE

1.

Construct the wax or clay nose as described above. After the nose is textured—and before coloring it with rubber mask grease—apply Vaseline with a ⅜″ brush over the entire surface, including several inches of the surrounding area, the eyelashes, and the eyebrows. If you have a mustache, as shown in the picture, use masking tape to cover and flatten it.

To ⅓ cup water add enough plaster of Paris to make a heavy, creamy, thick paste. (If you use warm water, it will set faster. Just how warm depends on how fast or slow you can do the job.)

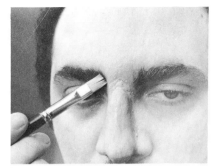
1

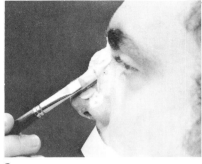
2

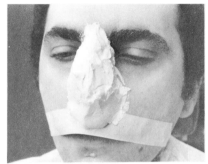
3

Make a test before attempting the actual application. Mix and smooth out the paste using your hand, a spatula, or a butter knife.

2–4.

Apply this paste to the nose and surrounding areas, using a ⅜″ brush. Make sure that the first layer is thin and that no air bubbles are trapped anywhere. Keep building at least a 1″ thickness all over, including the outer edges. At the last minute, fill up both nostrils and breathe through the mouth. (If you are casting a nose for someone else, explain the step by step process you will be using, including the closing of the nostrils, before beginning.) Smooth the paste all over with your finger or a spatula, and wait for it to dry. It will become hot before it sets, and then it will cool off.

5.

Using your hands, pull your muscles in opposite directions to separate them from the plaster.

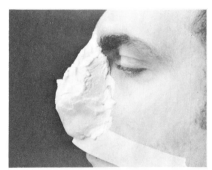
4

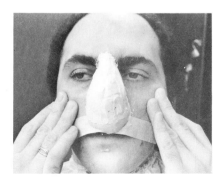
5

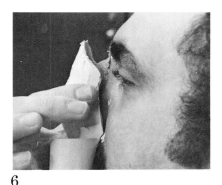

6

7

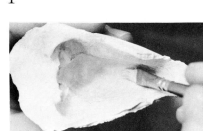

1

2

3

4

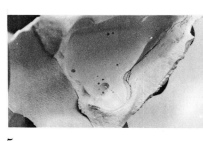

5

6.

Then gently remove the mold from the bridge of the nose.

7.

You now have the exact negative of the wax or clay nose you've created. Put this aside to dry (overnight, if possible) and clean your face.

To duplicate the new nose in latex you will need:

MATERIALS

1. Regular black or red pencil
2. Liquid latex
3. One ¾″ brush or a small Japanese brush
4. Hand hair dryer
5. Translucent powder and puff
6. Cake of soap
7. Paper towel
8. Cup of water

PROCEDURE

1.

Using a pencil, mark the actual size of the new nose inside the mold—that is, where the nose ends.

2–4.

There are two techniques you can use. With the first, the latex is brushed layer by layer inside the mold (drying each layer before proceeding), until the desired thickness is achieved.

5.

With the second technique, a small amount of latex is poured inside the mold up to the pencil-marked areas.

6.

Pour the leftover latex back into the cup via the lower part of the nose, as shown (never from the bridge or the sides), until the last drop has been used. Then, as before, dry each layer with a hand hair dryer. Keep adding more layers until reaching the desired thickness. (In either case, make sure that the edges of the piece are very thin; otherwise the nose will not blend into the skin when you put it on.) The number of layers depends on which technique you are using and how thick or thin the latex is. To see how the technique works, make one set of noses—using perhaps three layers of latex at the edges and seven or eight layers for the rest—and record the number of layers used for each area.

7.

Before removing the latex (it's best to let it dry overnight), powder the inside of the mold.

8.

Gently loosen an edge and remove the rest with a small brush dipped in powder. Be careful that the thin edges are not folded, rolled, or ripped.

9–10.

Gently cut out the nostrils and the new latex nose is ready for application.

When using a brush, follow these simple steps to protect it: dip the brush in water and rub it over a cake of soap; gently wipe the soapy brush over a paper towel to remove excess water, dip it into the latex, and paint the mold; after each layer, rinse the brush in water and repeat the procedure.

6

7

8

9

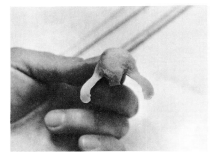

10

Latex Nose Application

To apply the latex nose you will need:

MATERIALS

1. Translucent powder and puff
2. Spirit gum
3. Liquid latex or Duo surgical adhesive
4. ⅛″ brush
5. Foam rubber sponge
6. Hand hair dryer
7. Rubber mask grease
8. Foundation
9. Red-A Creme Stick
10. Stipple sponge
11. Alcohol

APPLICATION

1.
Place the latex nose over your own nose, hold it in place, and powder all around.

2.
Remove it; this is the area in which you'll apply spirit gum.

3.
Apply the spirit gum only where you know the latex nose touches your own nose.

4.
Gently place the latex nose back in place and press to hold. If there are areas you have missed or some that require more spirit gum, use a small brush to get underneath and glue them down gently. (Liquid latex or Duo surgical adhesive can be used to glue on the nose instead of spirit gum, if you wish; the technique is the same.)

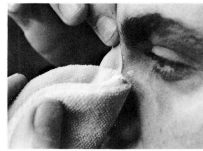

1

2

3

4

5.

When all the edges are glued down, go over the entire nose— and about ⅛″ beyond—with liquid latex, using a small piece of foam rubber sponge as an applicator.

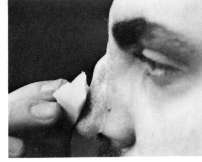

5

6.

Dry with a hand hair dryer and powder.

6

7.

Color it with the correct shade of rubber mask grease. (Mix the right shade, if you must, by combining several shades.)

7

8.

If you find, after applying the foundation, that the nose has a different tone than the rest of your face, stipple over it very gently with Red-A Creme Stick.

8

9.

Powder the entire face after your makeup is finished. Gently remove the latex nose, clean the spirit-gummed area with alcohol, or peel off the liquid latex (if you've used it) from the inside. Since the nose is already colored there's no need to color it again, but, after gluing it on the next time, repairs should be made at the edges so the whole piece blends into the rest of the skin. Instead of going over the entire nose with liquid latex, just a touch on the "seam" will be sufficient to blend and seal it.

Now that you have the mold, you can make as many new latex noses as you need for the run of the show.

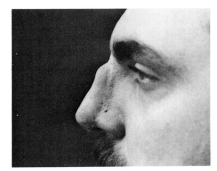

9

10

Applying a New Chin

The shape of your chin can be changed by using the same technique as that for the nose. (This change is basically for a short or weak chin.) See what it can do to the face in photographs (E–H) at the beginning of this chapter.

To make a chin longer or stronger, you will need:

MATERIALS

1. Spirit gum
2. Wax
3. Spatula or butter knife
4. Cup of water
5. Cold cream
6. ⅜″ brush
7. Sealer
8. Stipple sponge, foam rubber sponge
9. Rubber mask grease
10. Red-A Creme Stick
11. Creme Stick SC-50 or Beard Stubble Black

Begin with an idea for the shape and size of a chin appropriate to the character you'll be portraying. If necessary, keep a sketch of it in front of you.

APPLICATION

1.

Apply spirit gum over the chin and wait until it becomes tacky. This can be speeded up or tested by tapping the spirit gum a few times with the tip of your finger.

2.

Place a small amount of wax over the spirit gum, press down firmly, and spread to cover the gummy area. Now begin modeling. More wax can be added, if necessary, as you go along. *Do*

1

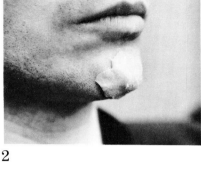

2

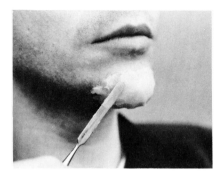

3

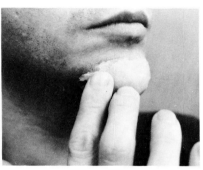

4

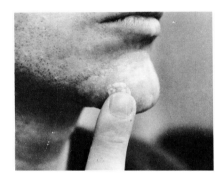

5

not begin with a large amount of wax; this will only create more trouble.

3–4.

Use your fingers (or a spatula or butter knife) for modeling. Since your fingers will become sticky, dip them in water as often as possible.

5.

After the modeling has been finished to your satisfaction, the whole surface can be smoothed by dipping the tips of your fingers in cold cream. (This, however, should be used very sparingly.)

6.

Using a ⅜″ brush, apply several layers of sealer on top of the wax. Wait until it dries before proceeding.

7.

Texture can be created by pressing a stipple sponge gently over the sealed wax.

8.

Color with rubber mask grease, using a foam rubber sponge as an applicator. Blend this color into the foundation, which should be the same shade.

9.

If you find that the color of the wax chin does not match your foundation, use a stipple sponge to apply a gentle, sparing touch of Red-A Creme Stick. Light touches of SC-50 or Beard Stubble Black can be added over this to achieve a "five o'clock shadow" effect.

10–11.

The final result.

If you are performing for more than one night, this process can become tedious; furthermore, there's no guarantee that you'll be able to duplicate your efforts. The wax chin, therefore, must be permanently duplicated in latex, following the same procedure explained on pages 124–26.

For film and television a professional makeup artist would not use any of the techniques explained here, but would make the new nose or chin with foam latex. Although there are times when a latex nose can be used

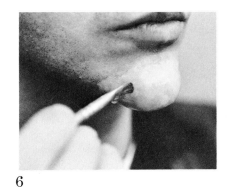

6

7

8

9

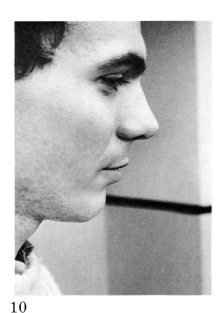

10

11

successfully, it must be a very well-made piece, with the thin edges blended carefully and with special attention given to the texture and coloring.

23

Scars

Scar with Scar Material

MATERIALS

1. Bottle of Scar Material
2. Basic foundation
3. Men's lip color (gray, red, and flesh color)
4. Tweezers or cotton and acetone

APPLICATION

Before applying Scar Material to your face, make a patch test to find out how your skin reacts. (Do not use it around the eyes, on children, or on very sensitive skin.)

1.

Make sure your skin is clean, and then apply a few layers of Scar Material in the shape desired. Let it dry. Additional layers should be applied if you need a deeper cut.

2.

When it dries you'll have a deep cut in the skin. Now apply your basic foundation. Since the natural color of the indented scar is similar to men's lip color, a bit of gray mixed into the red, plus a touch of flesh color, will give the best results.

1

2

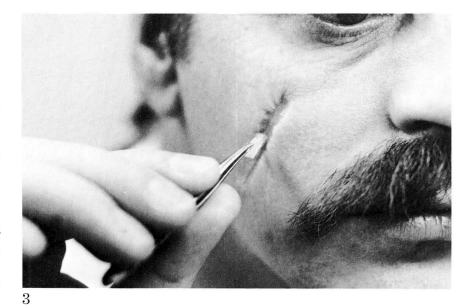

3

3.

To remove the scar, either peel it off with tweezers or dissolve it with cotton saturated in acetone. If you use acetone, make sure it doesn't get into your eyes. And if you have very sensitive skin, don't use it at all.

Scar with Premade Latex or Plastic Material

MATERIALS

1. Pre-made scar
2. Spirit gum or liquid latex
3. ⅛" brush
4. Acetone
5. Foam rubber sponge
6. Hand hair dryer
7. Translucent powder and puff
8. Rubber mask grease (same shade as the foundation)
9. Stage blood, if needed

APPLICATION

1.

Apply liquid latex or spirit gum to a clean area of the skin without going beyond the size of the scar desired.

2.

Place the latex scar over the adhesive and hold until secure. If more adhesive is required at the edges, apply it with a ⅛" brush. Any thin edges should be blended into the skin. If you're using a scar made of plastic, you can actually dissolve the edges into the skin with acetone.

3.

Using the foam rubber sponge as an applicator, apply a layer of liquid latex over the scar and about ⅛" beyond.

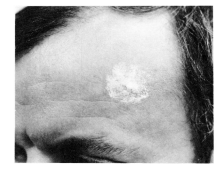
1

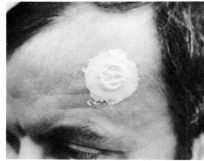
2

4.

Dry with a hand hair dryer, and then powder. Color with rubber mask grease the same shade as the foundation, and—if you need to—add a touch of stage blood. To remove the scar, gently loosen one section, lift, clean it with alcohol (especially where you've used spirit gum), and save it for the next performance.

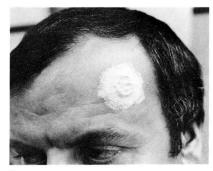
3

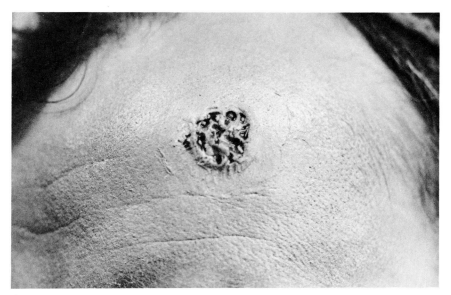
4

Scar with Creepy Skin

MATERIALS

1. Piece of Creepy Skin (this is a special wax mixed with cotton that remains soft and pliable. You can cut it to any size, mold it to any shape, and use it anywhere, from a shapeless nose to "cauliflower" ears.)
2. Spatula or butter knife

APPLICATION

1.

Take a piece of Creepy Skin, cut it to the desired size, and place it where you want a scar. Press down firmly. (It is advisable to start with clean skin.)

2–3.

Smooth and blend the edges with your fingers, with the spatula, or with a butter knife.

4.

Color it, if necessary, to get the desired effect.

To remove the scar, just pull it off and place it back in the jar or box. If you have to duplicate the shape, remove it gently and try to place it in the same area when using it again.

5–6.

If you're changing the shape of your nose or creating "cauliflower" ears, follow the same technique.

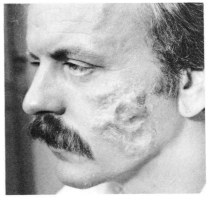

1

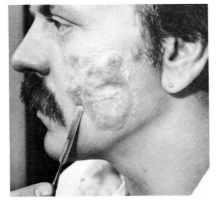

2

3

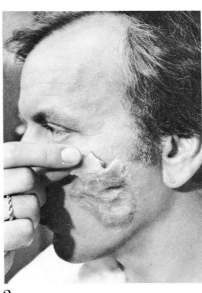

4

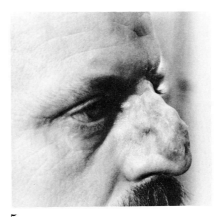

5

6

Scar with Gelatin

For something a little more permanent, try using gelatin and cotton.

MATERIALS

1. One package of Knox gelatin
2. Hot water
3. Ball of cotton
4. Spatula
5. Liquid latex
6. Foam rubber sponge
7. Translucent powder and puff
8. Foundation

APPLICATION

1.
Dissolve the gelatin as quickly as possible in hot water (one teaspoon of water to a package).

2.
Open up the ball of cotton, flatten it, and mix it with the gelatin.

3.
As soon as the cotton is well saturated, place it on your face (or wherever it goes), press down firmly, shape it with a spatula, and blend the edges to the skin.

4.
When the gelatin has set, apply a coat of liquid latex over it using a foam rubber sponge as an applicator. Let the latex dry, and then powder.

5.
Apply your basic foundation and color.

6.
Gently remove the scar. The shape will hold (the latex keeps it together), although it will shrink a little after drying completely.

When using the gelatin scar again, apply liquid latex to the back or to your skin, and simply place it on. Hold until secure, especially at the edges.

1

2

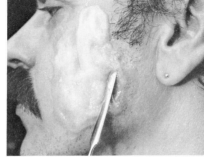
3

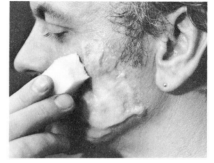
4

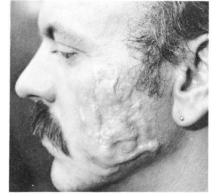
5

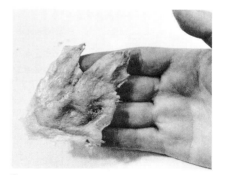
6

Scar with Wax

MATERIALS

1. Spirit gum
2. ⅜" brush
3. Wax
4. Spatula
5. Cup of water
6. Cold cream
7. Sealer
8. Acetone
9. Stipple sponge, foam rubber sponge
10. Red-A Creme Stick
11. Rubber mask grease
12. Translucent powder and puff
13. Stage blood

APPLICATION

1.

Take a ⅜" brush and apply spirit gum to the area where you want a scar. Wait until it becomes gummy.

2.

Place a small amount of wax on top and press to hold. (Try to start with a small amount; you can always add more if necessary.)

3.

With the tip of your finger or a spatula, shape and thin out the edges of the wax so it blends to the skin. (Since wax is a sticky substance, you'll frequently find it necessary to dip your finger in water or cold cream. The cold cream, however, should be used only sparingly.)

4.

When you're satisfied with the size and shape of the scar, apply a layer or two of sealer on top and let it dry. (While it's drying, clean your brush in acetone.)

1

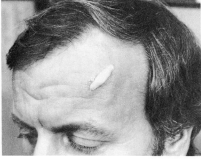
2

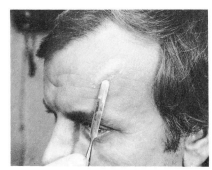
3

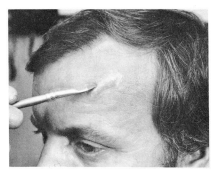
4

5.

Gently go over the sealed wax with a stipple sponge to give it some skin texture.

6.

Using a foam rubber sponge as an applicator, color the scar with rubber mask grease, the same shade as the foundation, and then powder. If you don't like the color, you can stipple it with a touch of Red-A Creme Stick.

7.

A cut in the wax can be created with the end of a brush, the tip of an orange stick, a spatula, or any other tool that is not sharp.

8.

A few drops of stage blood will create a fresh, bloody scar. If the blood gathers into drops, powder before application.

This scar cannot be reused. To remove it, simply scrape it off with a spatula, rinse off the blood, and save the wax for a future use.

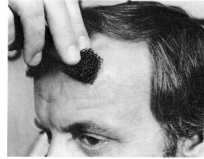

5

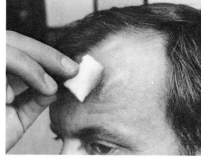

6

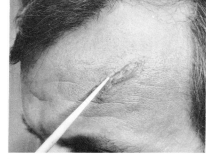

7

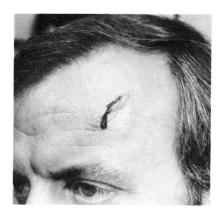

8

Scar with Cotton

MATERIALS

1. Spirit gum
2. Ball of cotton
3. Liquid latex
4. Foam rubber sponge
5. Tweezers
6. Hand hair dryer
7. Translucent powder and puff
8. Rubber mask grease
9. ⅛" brush
10. Red-A Creme Stick
11. Stipple sponge
12. Acetone or alcohol

APPLICATION

1.
Apply spirit gum to the area where you want a scar. When this is gummy, place the cotton on top and press to hold.

2.
Remove any excess cotton.

3.
Saturate the remaining cotton with liquid latex, using a foam rubber sponge as an applicator.

4.
Shape the wet cotton into the desired shape with tweezers.

5.
Dry with a hand hair dryer.

6.
Powder.

1

2

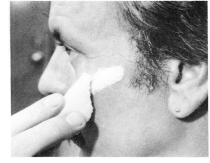

3

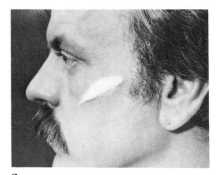

4

5

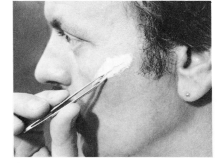

6

7.

Color with a shade of rubber mask grease that matches the foundation.

8.

Use a ⅛″ brush to color the inside folds and crevices, if necessary.

9.

If the color of the scar is different from the foundation, simply stipple on a touch of Red-A Creme Stick. To remove the scar, loosen one corner and peel it off. Use acetone or alcohol to clean the spirit gum from your face.

The careful application of scar material, wax, and ready-made scars with latex should give you successful results for use in television and film. A lot of fine, detailed work is absolutely necessary if you're using other techniques, especially when texturing, coloring, and blending edges to the skin.

7

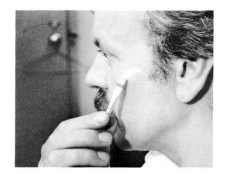

8

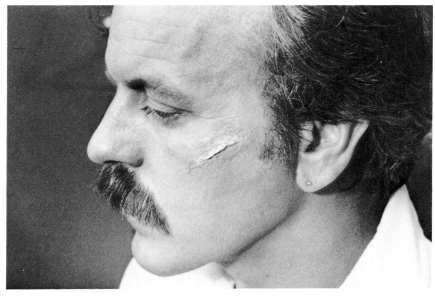

9

24

Oriental Makeup

For this makeup you will need someone to help you.

MATERIALS

1. Pair of Oriental eyelids
2. Translucent powder and puff
3. Liquid latex
4. Foam rubber sponge
5. Spatula
6. Hand hair dryer
7. Rubber mask grease
8. Foundation
9. Highlight (a few shades lighter than the foundation)
10. Shading (a few shades darker than the foundation)
11. Natural or synthetic fibers
12. Spirit gum
13. One or two makeup brushes

APPLICATION

1.

Oriental eyelids must be large enough to cover the area from your eyelashes to your eyebrows, and from one corner of the eye to the other. Any other size will create a problem.

2.

Place the eyelid latex piece so you can look straight ahead easily and without discomfort.

1

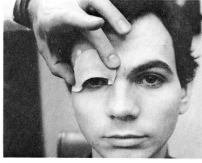

2

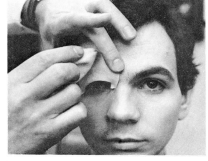

3

4

3–4.

Holding it in place, powder heavily all around so that when the piece is lifted you will know where to reposition it.

5.

Using a small piece of foam rubber sponge, apply liquid latex inside that frame. Don't get any into your eyebrows or eyelashes, and stay away from your eyelids.

5

6.
Take the eyelid piece and gently reposition it inside the frame. Press to adhere.

7.
If some areas here and there have been missed, use a thin brush or spatula to add a touch of liquid latex under the eyelid piece.

8.
Do the same with the other eye.

9–10.
Using a foam rubber sponge as an applicator, cover both pieces with a layer of liquid latex. If the edges are obvious or not thin enough, add a few layers of latex to blend them with the skin.

11.
Dry with a hand hair dryer.

12.
Powder.

13.
Apply rubber mask grease the same shade as the foundation.

6

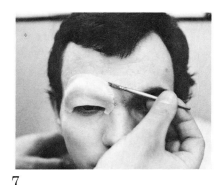
7

8

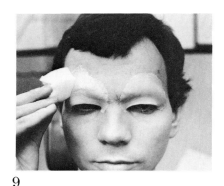
9

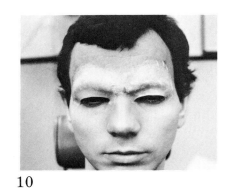
10

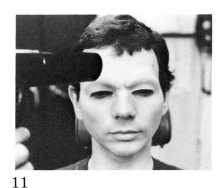
11

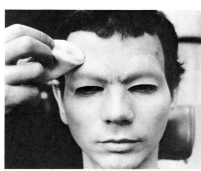
12

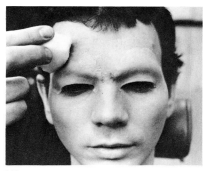
13

14

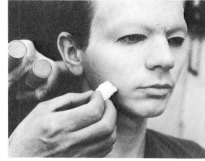

15

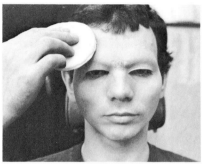

16

17

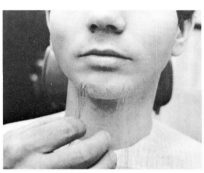

18

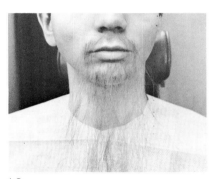

19

14.
Blend foundation over the forehead and a little highlight over the cheekbone.

15.
Add some shading under the cheekbone to create a thin face.

16.
Powder the entire face.

17.
If your character requires a beard and mustache, buy them ready-made, or lay on natural or synthetic fibers as follows. After pouring several drops of spirit gum or liquid latex on the table, take a few hairs at a time (three or four to be exact) and press the tips into the gum or latex.

18.
Cover the chin—underneath and around it.

19.
Add the same long hairs for the mustache. The entire beard and mustache should be thin and sparse.

20–22.

With the proper clothes and mannerisms (walking, sitting, speaking), you can achieve a believable Oriental appearance. Remember that the highlight and shading used here are suited to this particular actor's bone structure. If you have a very healthy, full face, changing it to a thin one with high cheekbones and shading will not be easy—you might simply wind up with a dirty face. (Remember, too, that not all Orientals are thin!) Do the best you can with your face and stay away from stereotypes.

23–24.

This effect was achieved using the same Oriental eyelids and the same techniques, plus the addition of an appropriate hairstyle and costume.

These latex pieces have been used in television and film with great success. Extreme care is necessary, however, in choosing pieces that are the correct size, and in texturing, coloring, and blending the thin edges.

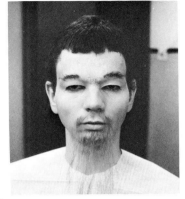

20

21

22

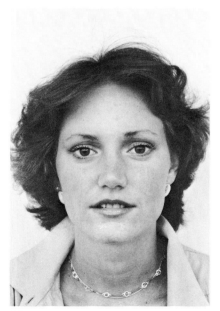

23

24

Simulated Oriental Makeup

This approach is not suitable for actors with very deep-set eyes.

MATERIALS

1. Cake eyeliner, black or brown
2. Eyeliner brush
3. Eyebrow pencil, black or brown
4. White or highlight (a few shades lighter than the foundation)
5. ¾″ brush
6. Translucent powder and puff
7. Rouge
8. Lipstick

APPLICATION

1.

Using cake eyeliner and an eyeliner brush—or a very sharp eyebrow pencil the same shade as the eyeliner—extend your usual eye line approximately half an inch downwards, towards your nose.

2.

Take a ¾″ brush and apply white or highlight all over your eyelids, as close to the eyeliner and your eyebrows as possible. Powder. If applied correctly, you will have very puffy eyelids.

3.

Depending on their present shape, your eyebrows can be changed to a pair that are short and thick, long and thin, arched, or even straight. A little observation and research goes a long way.

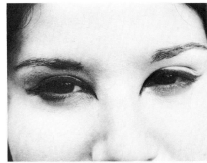

1

2

3

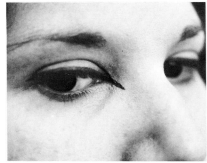

4

4.

The end result is simulated Oriental eye makeup. Apply your foundation, blend the edges of your eye makeup, powder the entire face, add rouge and lipstick, and then, by adding appropriate hairstyle, costume, and Oriental mannerisms, you can achieve a believable appearance.

 Bald Cap

For this makeup you will need someone to help you.

MATERIALS

1. Bald cap
2. Comb
3. Pencil
4. Scissors
5. Spirit gum
6. Liquid latex or Duo surgical adhesive
7. Foam rubber sponge
8. Hand hair dryer
9. Translucent powder and puff
10. Rubber mask grease
11. Foundation
12. Red-A Creme Stick
13. Black stipple sponge
14. Beard Stubble Black
15. Natural, synthetic, or crepe hair
16. Paper towel
17. Beard stubble adhesive
18. Assorted brushes (eyebrow brush, powder brush, one or two makeup brushes)
19. Alcohol

2

1

3

APPLICATION

1.

Start with a clean face. Comb your hair back, making it as flat as possible.

2.

Place the bald cap comfortably on your head, making sure your sideburns and temples are well covered. (If your sideburns are long, either trim them or get a different-sized cap.)

3.

Mark the cap as close to the hairline as possible, about 1″ on the forehead and back of the neck and ¼″ around the temples and sideburns.

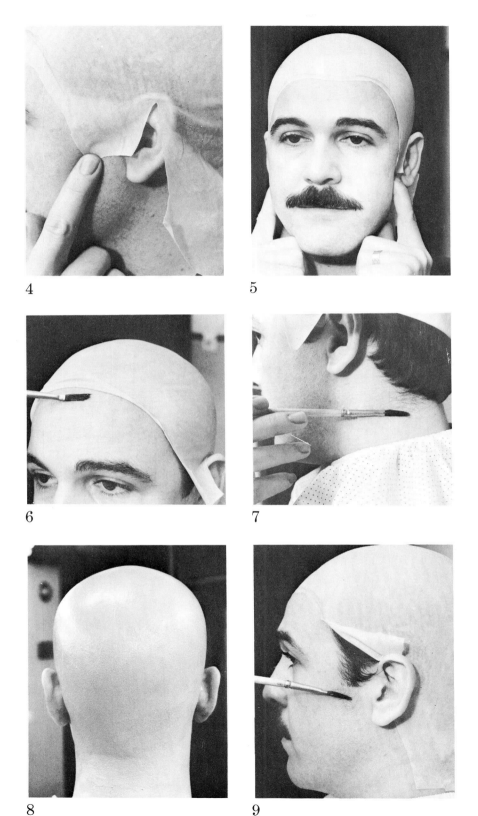

4

5

6

7

8

9

4.

Cut off the excess latex in front and in back. Do not cut the mark for the ear all the way up—stop just about ½″ before reaching the top, so that when you throw the cap behind, it will hug the ear.

5.

Before gluing, make sure the cap is in its proper place.

6.

Lift up the front of the cap and apply spirit gum to your forehead, perhaps as far back as your hairline but not beyond the edge of the cap. (If your hairline is very thick, do not glue the cap all the way up to the hairline, as this will create a ridge.) Make sure the front is thoroughly glued by lifting the edge of the cap several times, until the adhesive is gummy. Then replace the cap and press to hold.

7–8.

Lift the back and glue the cap from one side to the other. (Long hair should be trimmed; if not, at least leave enough of the cap to cover it.) Before gluing the back, make sure that your head is an inch or so higher than normal eye level; hold in this position during the gluing, until the cap is secure. Otherwise the cap could wrinkle in the back.

9.

Now glue each sideburn. If the cap is cut well, it will fit perfectly. If not, you'll have to stretch it a little to get rid of the unwanted wrinkles. There are three sides you must glue—the front of the sideburns, the back next to the ears, and the bottom.

10.

After all sides are dry, go over the entire cap and ¼″ beyond the edges with liquid latex or Duo surgical adhesive, using a foam rubber sponge as an applicator.

11.

Dry with a hand hair dryer.

12.

Do not touch the cap. Look in the mirror. If the front edge is thick, and it's obvious you're wearing one, go over the edge with a few layers of liquid latex, drying each layer before applying the next.

13.

Powder the entire head and brush off the excess.

14.

Choose a shade of rubber mask grease that matches your foundation and apply it evenly and smoothly over the entire head, using a foam rubber sponge as an applicator.

15.

Powder the cap again, but do not rub. Just pat and brush off the excess.

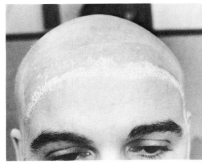

10

11

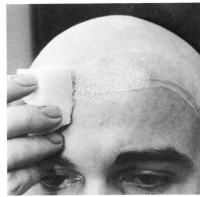

12

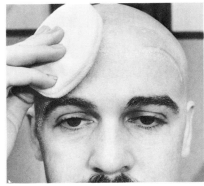

13

14

15

16

17

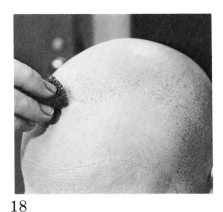

18

19

21

20

16–17.

Take a good look at yourself after applying foundation and coloring. If you find that the cap needs toning, use a black stipple sponge and carefully apply Red-A Creme Stick, which will remedy the "flat" look.

Your character is either totally bald or he has shaved his entire head. If he is clean shaven, he should have a five o'clock shadow all over. If he is bald on top, he should have the five o'clock shadow around the sides of his head.

18.

If your character has a shaved head, use a clean black stipple sponge to apply Beard Stubble Black, gently touching the cap in areas where there would be hair growth normally.

19–21.

The end result is a shaved head with a so-called "five o'clock shadow." If you need one or two days' growth on the head, take natural, synthetic, or crepe hair of different shades and cut it over a paper towel into lengths no longer than ¹/₁₆″.

22.

Rub beard stubble adhesive over the cap or just along the sides. Use your fingertips to smooth out any lumps.

23.

Press a foam rubber sponge over the cut hairs, and then press these firmly onto the adhesive. If the hair becomes lumpy in some areas, remove the excess with an eyebrow brush.

24.

The end result should look as natural as possible. If not, a little homework is necessary.

A lot of perspiration under the cap can cause it to loosen and pucker. If this happens, simply dry the wetness and re-glue.

If you're getting heavy wrinkles at the back of the neck when turning your head to the side, either the cap is too big or else it's not glued properly. Noticing this on stage, however, is a bit too late—just don't turn your back on the audience!

To remove your cap, pry it gently from the back of the neck using a brush dipped in alcohol. Do the sideburns after the back is released, and then, throwing the cap over your face, gently remove it. Clean off the spirit gum with alcohol and a cloth, and place the cap on a wig block. Before the next performance simply put it on and glue it into place. Since it's already colored, just stipple a band of liquid latex all around. Then dry, powder, match the coloring, and touch up here and there if necessary.

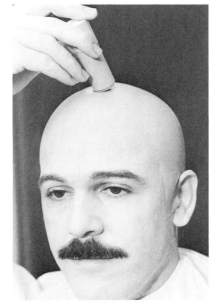

22

23

24

A theatrical bald cap cannot be used for film or television since it's designed to last for more than one performance and is simply too thick. Photographs 25 and 26 depict the thickness of the theatrical bald cap and the thinness of the film and television bald cap respectively; in the latter you can even see the subject's hair showing through.

To apply the bald cap for film and television, follow the same steps as described above, but omit trimming the front or back sections. Although this cap has very thin edges, it is still important to dissolve them so they'll blend into the skin and become a continuous part of your forehead.

27–30.

After gluing the entire cap (steps 6–9), take a clean brush, dip it in acetone, and place it over the excess pieces left unglued (if any) and all around the very edges of the cap. Press and hold for a few seconds; you will see that the acetone dissolves the edges to virtually nothing. As a result, they cannot be seen by the naked eye or the eye of a camera. From this point on, pick up where you left off—i.e., step 9, and continue with step 10, the application of liquid latex. Since this cap cannot be used more than once, you must keep enough of them on hand for the duration of the film or tape. Even if it's only for one show, make sure you have at least one or two extra caps available in case of accident.

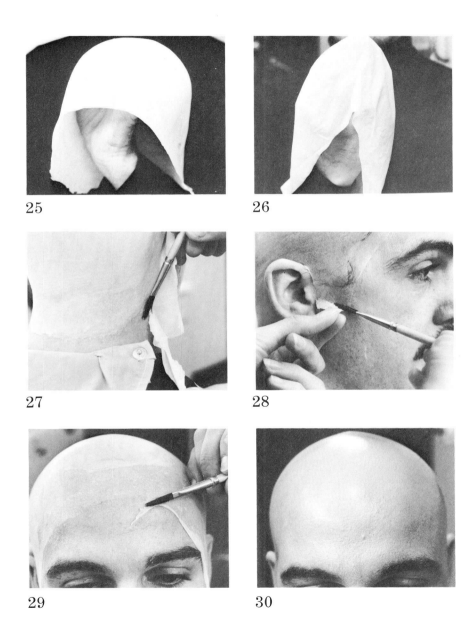

25

26

27

28

29

30

31–32.

If desired, five o'clock shadow or hair growth can be created on this cap as explained in steps 18 to 23.

33–34.

"Before" and "after."

When applying all the prosthetic pieces and bald caps for television and film, Plastic Adhesive can be used instead of spirit gum. It is strong and resistant to sweat and stress. To use this material:

• Comb the subject's hair flat.

• Place the cap, fit it, and fold the front section back, exposing the hair.

• Paint one layer of Plastic Adhesive over the folded area. Dry, powder, and dust off any excess powder. Leave that section alone and proceed to the next step.

• Apply one layer of adhesive over the forehead. Dry, powder, and remove the excess powder. In both sections, *do not* apply more than one layer of adhesive. Don't go beyond where the cap is to be applied, and be careful not to get Plastic Adhesive in the subject's hair.

• Bring the folded section down over the forehead very carefully and press to hold. Adhesion is instant and strong.

• Follow the same procedure for the sideburns and the back of the neck.

• Dissolve the edges of the cap to the skin with acetone, and continue as explained above with bald cap.

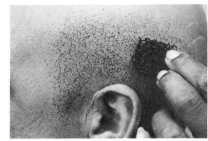

31

32

33

34

26

Covering Eyebrows with Wax and Latex

This is done at specific times for certain characters, nationalities, and periods—i.e., if you are in a period play where fashion dictates very thin, arched eyebrows, or if you must change your eyebrows for Oriental eyes.

There are several techniques you can use, and these involve wax, latex, plastic, nylon, silk, or foam rubber. The simplest, I think, is wax or latex.

Wax Eyebrow Cover

MATERIALS

1. Spirit gum
2. Silk or nylon cloth
3. Comb
4. Wax
5. Spatula or butter knife
6. Sealer
7. ¾" brush, eyeliner brush
8. Acetone
9. Rubber mask grease
10. Foam rubber sponge
11. Translucent powder and puff
12. Cake eyeliner, brown or black

APPLICATION

1.
If your eyebrows are very thick, saturate them first with spirit gum. Press them down as flat as you can, using silk or nylon cloth, and comb the hairs to separate and to prevent lumpiness. (Dampen the cloth, if necessary.) Then proceed as for thin eyebrows, taking a small amount of wax, using a spatula or butter knife to cover the hairs. Press down to get a very flat surface, and comb and separate the brows, if necessary.

2.
Go over the waxed eyebrows with several layers of sealer. Let each layer dry before adding the next. Do not rub back and forth, but make a smooth movement from one end to another. Use a ¾" brush and, while waiting for the sealer to dry, rinse it out in acetone.

3.
With a foam rubber sponge as an applicator, cover the eyebrows with the right shade of rubber mask grease to match the foundation.

4.
Powder.

5.
The end result.

1

2

3

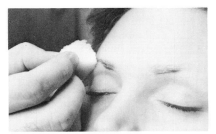

4

5

6–9.

Do not draw a hard line with an eyebrow pencil and call it an eyebrow. Use instead a thin, sharp eyeliner brush and cake eyeliner (brown or black), creating the desired shape and style with tiny lines—feather strokes—placed side by side. Do not be dismayed if the thickness of the eyebrows shows. If this is too obvious, however, try other materials and techniques.

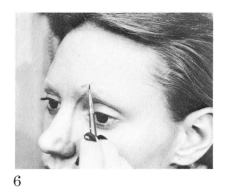

6

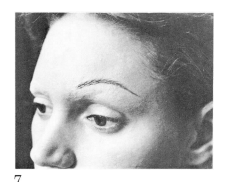

7

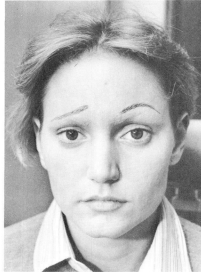

8

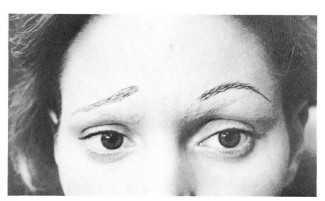

9

Latex Eyebrow Cover

MATERIALS

1. Regular pencil
2. Liquid latex
3. ⅜" brush, ⅛" brush
4. Cup of water
5. Cake of soap
6. Paper towels
7. Translucent powder and puff
8. Spirit gum
9. Comb
10. Silk cloth or spatula
11. Rubber mask grease
12. Ready-made brows or braided crepe hair (optional)

APPLICATION

1.

Draw the shape and size of the eyebrows on a clean surface, making sure this outline is about ¼" wider and longer than your own brows.

2.

Brush layers of liquid latex inside the pattern, drying each layer as you go along. There should be five or six layers at the center of the pattern, tapering to two or three at the edges. (To save your brush, dip it first in water, then run it over a cake of soap, and press over a paper towel before dipping it in the latex. Clean your brush this way after each layer.)

1

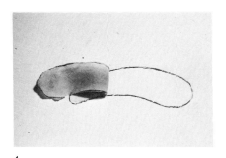

2

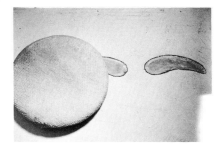

3

4

3–4.

When dry, powder and lift up the eyebrows. Reverse the sides, using the left side for the right eyebrow and the right side for the left eyebrow. (This means the pieces are turned over. The back side of any latex piece is usually not as shiny as the front side.)

5–8.

Apply spirit gum over your eyebrows and about ¼″ beyond. Separate the hairs with a comb and press with a silk cloth or spatula, making them as flat as possible.

9–10.

Place the latex piece and press to adhere. If there are any loose edges, go under them with spirit gum using a ⅛″ brush.

11–12.

Cover the latex piece with a layer of latex. Dry and powder.

5

6

7

8

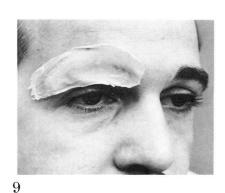

9

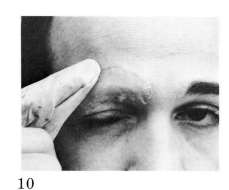

10

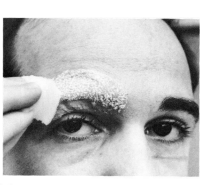

11

12

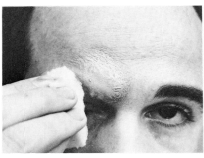

13

14

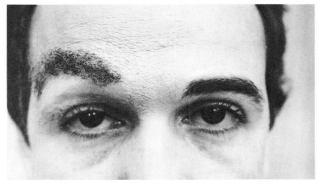

15

13.

Color with rubber mask grease the same shade as the foundation.

14–15.

Draw the new eyebrow on top, as explained above in steps 6 to 9 of Wax Eyebrow Cover, or glue on ready-made brows with spirit gum or liquid latex. Or, take some braided crepe hair and open it, comb out the kinks, and separate two pieces the size of the eyebrows you need. Roll them individually in the palms of your hands, and glue them over the eyebrow cover with liquid latex.

The two techniques explained here should be adequate in helping you create the effect you're after. Both can be used for television and film, except for the crepe hair eyebrows. That's where the wigmaker comes in—he makes you a pair with natural hair over thin lace.

27

Lifts Their Construction and Use

Lifts are used to pull up sagging muscles (i.e., jaws, eyelids, neck) and to smooth the skin for a more youthful appearance. This procedure is somewhat easier for women than men, since women generally have longer hair and are thus better able to conceal the lift apparatus. If men use it, certain changes in hair style (or the addition of a hair piece, if bald, or sideburns) may be necessary.

For the application of the lift you will need someone to help you.

MATERIALS

1. Flesh-colored silk or nylon
2. Heavy-duty black, brown, or white thread (depending on the hair color)
3. Two very small rubber bands
4. Tube of Duco cement
5. One hook and eye set (the eye is not necessary)
6. Liquid latex or Duo surgical adhesive
7. Alcohol
8. Hand hair dryer
9. Hair clips, bobby pins
10. Comb
11. Makeup appropriate for your character

1

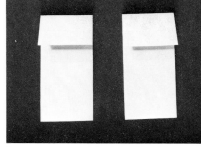

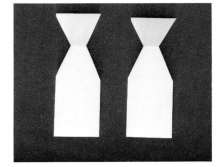
2

CONSTRUCTION

1.
Cut two rectangular pieces of silk or nylon approximately ¾″ wide and 2″ long.

2.
Fold over each piece about ½″ from one end.

3

3.
Cut a small triangle from each of the folded corners.

4.
Cut two sections of thread, each about 3″ long, form them into loops, and tie them to the rubber bands.

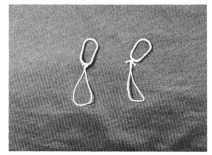
4

5.
Pass the silk or nylon pieces you have prepared (step 3) through the thread loops, and fold over the flaps. Place them on a smooth surface (such as a mirror) and glue down the flaps with Duco cement.

5

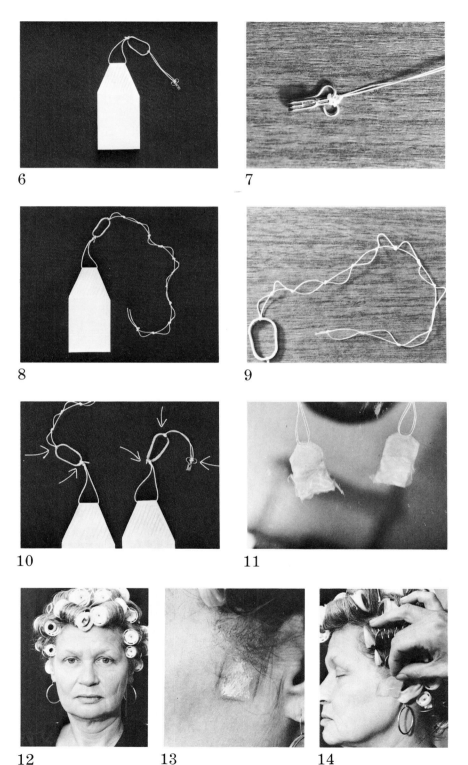

6

7

8

9

10

11

12

13

14

6–7.

When dry, take one of the pieces and add an inch or two of the same colored thread to the opposite end of the rubber band. Then knot the end of the thread to the hook.

8–9.

Take the other piece and attach a 7″ loop of thread to the opposite end of the rubber band. As shown, knot smaller loops every ¼″.

10–11.

Place both pieces over the table and secure each knot (shown at the arrows) with a touch of Duco cement; saturate the silk sections with liquid latex or Duo surgical adhesive only if you are ready to use the lifts.

12.

Set your hair now, if necessary.

13.

Clean the "sideburn" area with alcohol, and then apply liquid latex or Duo surgical adhesive to a 1″ by ¾″ patch. If you're in a hurry, dry the latex with a hand hair dryer. When dry it will become transparent.

14.

Remove the lifts from the mirror, one at a time, and gently place them on top of the dried liquid latex.

15.

Make sure both lifts are glued to the face at the same angle and in the exact direction where pull is desired. A mistake at this point can't be corrected simply by lifting the pieces and replacing them in a different area.

16.

Finish the makeup and remove any curlers. (The makeup, of course, should correspond to the age of the character and the period in which he lives.)

17.

Open a part on top of the head from ear to ear. Comb each section to the front and to the back, securing it with hair clips.

18.

Make a pincurl at the center of the part. (Without this pincurl you can't be sure the lifts will stay in place for any length of time. The line might slip down and, of course, the facial muscles with it.)

19–20.

Holding each line, look in the mirror and pull up as far as possible without creating unwanted wrinkles around the eyes and neck.

21.

When you're sure where the two lines should be attached, hook them together in front of the pincurl, adding an extra bobby pin for security.

22.

When totally satisfied, comb and dress the hair to cover the lines and pincurl. After bringing down two pieces of hair to cover the nylon lifts on the sideburn areas, the job is done.

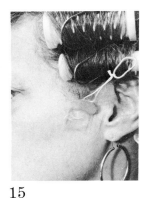

15

16

17

18

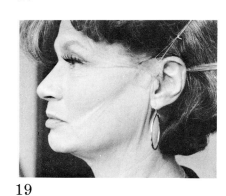

19

20

21

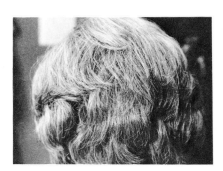

22

23.

"Before," the model as herself.

24–25.

"After," completed makeup full face and profile. The tension will be felt for only a few minutes; it will not prevent you from moving and opening your mouth freely.

If you need to be your own age again during the course of the production, simply cut or un-hook the line at the top of your head and let your muscles relax into their original place.

If sagging eyebrows need to be lifted, glue two lifts on your forehead, each an inch or so away from your eyebrows. After making two pincurls on top of the head, bring up the lines and wrap them around the pincurls until the proper tension is main-tained. In this case each lift should have only a long double line, not a hook, and the rubber band should be far enough from the silk or nylon so it's hidden under your hair. To cover this apparatus on your forehead, comb down some of your hair into bangs.

If loose neck muscles must be tightened, you'll have to use two lifts—one on each side of your neck near the hair growth. For this you won't need pincurls. Simply tie the two ends behind your neck and cover the lifts with the proper hairdo.

Use alcohol or makeup remover to remove these lifts. Although none of them should be used again, the lines, hooks, and rubber bands can be saved. For

23

24

best results, however, replace the used pieces of silk or nylon with new ones.

Since the entire lift mechanism is underneath the hair, it can be used very successfully in television and film. But do be careful about watching how far you pull up your muscles— you don't want to overdo it and look ridiculous in front of those cameras.

25

28

Odds and Ends

Sunburn, Moles, Droopy Eyelids, Freckles, Liver Spots, Perspiration, Tears, Blood, Cuts and Bruises, Teeth, Acne, Burns and Blisters, Diseased Hand, Blind Eye

Sunburn

This process is for creating the peeling of skin after sunburn.

For the sunburn itself, depending on the color of your skin, you can use a very red tone with a touch of raw purple. For peeling you will need:

MATERIALS

1. Liquid latex
2. Foam rubber sponge
3. Hand hair dryer
4. Translucent powder and puff
5. Foundation
6. Tweezers
7. Scissors
8. Cream rouge (fleshtone red)

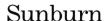

APPLICATION

1.
Apply a generous layer of liquid latex to the area (in this case, the forehead) using a foam rubber sponge as an applicator.

2.
Dry with a hand hair dryer until the latex becomes dry and transparent. Powder, apply the basic tan or sunburn foundation over the latex, and powder again.

3.
With either your finger or the help of a tweezers, gently pull away a section of the latex. It will look like a tent.

4.
While holding the tip, cut off the latex "tent" with scissors. It will snap back to create a hole.

5.
The size of each hole can be controlled by how far you pull the latex away from your forehead and how much of it you cut off. After you have enough holes, add a touch of red cream rouge (or a shade closest to fleshtone) inside each one.

1

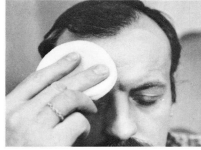

2

3

4

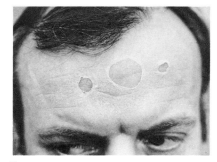

5

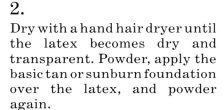

Moles

MATERIALS

1. Liquid latex
2. Smooth table or mirror

APPLICATION

1–2.

Sprinkle several drops of liquid latex over a smooth table or mirror. After allowing them to dry overnight, you'll have a variety of dried up "moles."

3.

After you've finished your makeup, add a touch of liquid latex or spirit gum to the back of each mole and glue it to your face.

4.

Color the moles, if you want to, or glue on a few hairs.

1

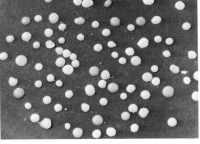
2

3

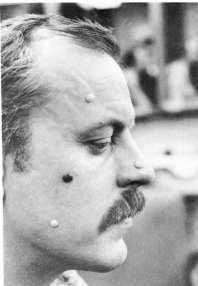
4

Droopy Eyelids

MATERIALS

1. Roll of Scotch-brand transparent tape (not the shiny type) 1″ wide
2. Scissors
3. Soap

APPLICATION

1–2.
Cut a piece of tape the length of your eyelid and shape it to cover the lid.

3–4.
Use soap and water to clean your eyelid of all natural oils and makeup, and then press the tape over it. Depending on how wide you've cut the tape, you'll get a closed or half-closed eyelid. There is no need to apply makeup over it, since the tape isn't shiny, but you can use a little if you wish.

5.
To remove the tape, simply loosen an outer corner and pull it off gently while holding or pulling your skin in the opposite direction.

1

2

3

4

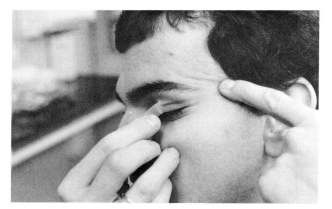

5

Freckles

MATERIALS

1. Light, medium, and dark lining colors
2. ⅛″ brush

APPLICATION

1.

Freckles usually appear on very fair, thin skins. They come in all shapes and sizes and, depending on how much time your character has spent in the sun, and what color his skin tone is, they can vary from light to dark brown. The darker the skin, the darker the freckles. Since they can be found anywhere—cheeks, forehead, nose, chin—there's no one part of the face to concentrate on.

2.

Choose a color, or mix a few colors, to get the right shade. Apply the freckles with a small brush, but don't make them all the same size and shape—they're not all round, square, or rectangular, nor do they have any definite outline. Observe others who have freckles to get the general idea.

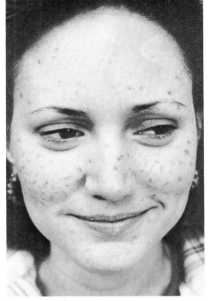

1

2

1

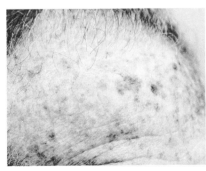

2

Liver Spots

MATERIALS

1. Gray violet 17 lining color
2. ⅛″ brush

APPLICATION

1–2.

Liver spots are a little larger than freckles. They appear late in life, as do different sizes of moles, but are not concentrated in one area and are not as numerous as freckles. Usually they're a dark brownish-purple, the color of liver, but—depending on the tone of your foundation—this color can change to a lighter or darker shade, or even to a brownish-gray or ash shade. When you have determined the right shade, apply these spots on the face and the backs of the hands with a brush.

Perspiration

MATERIALS

1. Tears and perspiration solution (glycerin)
2. Shallow dish

APPLICATION

1.

Pour a small amount of the solution into a shallow dish. After your makeup is completed, dip your fingers into the dish.

2–3.

Dab the solution all over your face, neck, and a touch at your hairline—depending on how much perspiration you need. If you do not rub or wash your face, the "perspiration" will stay on as long as you want it to.

1

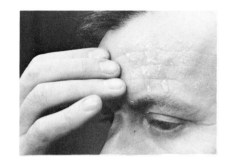

2

3

Tears

MATERIALS

1. Glycerin
2. Plastic eyedropper

APPLICATION

Needless to say, this must be done just before going on stage.

1.

Fill half an eyedropper with glycerin.

2.

Place the tip of the eyedropper at the inner corner of each eye—but not actually *in* the eye—and gently squeeze.

3.

The slow-moving glycerin—and your accompanying physical

coordination with the act of crying—will make this appear believable. If any glycerin gets into your eyes it will burn slightly, thus stimulating your tear ducts. Then you'll *really* cry.

An alternate method is to cry naturally (by getting into the mood of the character) or mechanically (by learning to have control over your muscles).

1

2

3

Blood
For external use

MATERIALS

1. Bottle of stage blood
2. Shallow dish
3. Piece of sponge (natural or synthetic)

APPLICATION

1.

Pour the theatrical blood into a shallow dish. Saturate a sponge with the blood and place it onstage where you can easily reach it without the audience noticing.

2.

When you get to the sponge, take it and squeeze as hard as you can.

3.

Your hand and fingers will become a bloody mess. Rehearse this several times before the actual performance. If you must get blood on your clothes, use water for practice.

4–6.

If you are entering the stage bleeding from a head wound, for instance, fill up a small or large syringe, place it on the spot, squeeze, and let the blood run.

1

2

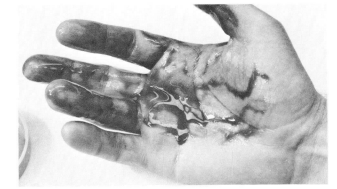

3

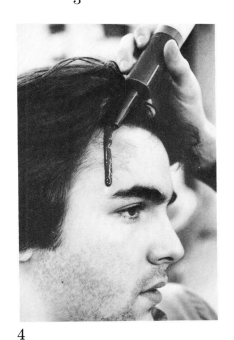

4

5

6

Blood

For internal use

MATERIALS

1. One empty capsule
2. Cherry or chocolate syrup, or theatrical blood for internal use

APPLICATION

1.

Open the capsule.

2.

Fill the longer half with the syrup of your choice.

3.

Close the capsule and carry it with you, or place it on the set where you can get to it easily.

4.

Put the capsule in your mouth, bite down when the time comes, and push the liquid out with your tongue. Swallow the soft capsule or dispose of it, so it won't be noticed by the audience. All this needs a little advance planning and timing. Under certain body and environmental temperatures the capsule will soften and break open. You must find out how soon it has to be filled and put into your mouth.

You can also use ready-made blood capsules by Leichner. These are filled with a special powdered foaming agent and color. The instant the capsule comes in contact with the saliva, it turns into red foam and can be spit out as blood.

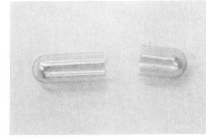

1

2

3

4

Cuts and Bruises

MATERIALS

1. Colors of red, blue, black, and white in Creme Stick or clown color kit
2. Foam rubber sponge
3. Three ⅜" brushes
4. Spirit gum
5. Wax
6. Spatula or butter knife
7. Sealer
8. Acetone
9. Toothpick or orange stick
10. Stage blood

APPLICATION

Mix red and blue colors to get the dark purplish bruise color, or use gray violet SL17. Play with these colors until you get the right shade.

1.

Using a small piece of foam rubber sponge, apply this shade around the eye and below the cheekbone, creating a semicircle under the cheekbone.

2.

With the tip of your finger or a brush, place a little white over the cheekbone and blend.

3–4.

Add a touch of black, if necessary, under the white area. If you work carefully, the effect will be a lump that is believable in close-ups as well as at a distance. For the real black-and-blue bruise, add a touch of black to the purple for the right tone.

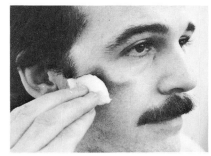

1

2

3

4

There are other stages of bruises you should be aware of. For the character you are portraying, find out which one is called for—it could be black-and blue, purple, green, or yellow.

If you need a cut over the bruise:

5.

Apply a touch of spirit gum to the predetermined area. Wait until it is gummy.

6.

Place a small amount of wax on top and, using a spatula or butter knife, shade and blend the edges.

7.

Add a layer of sealer on top of the wax. Clean your brush in acetone while waiting for the sealer to dry.

8.

For the cut itself, take the end of a toothpick, an orange stick, or a pencil, and create the cut.

9.

Add a drop or two of stage blood inside the cut for the best effect.

5

6

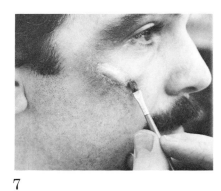

7

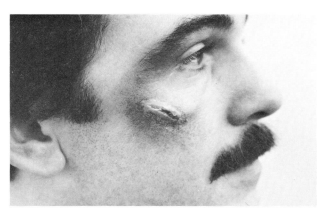

8

9

Teeth

To give the effect of chipped or missing teeth, use either black tooth enamel or a black eyebrow pencil. For yellowish-looking teeth, use a light or dark brown eyebrow pencil.

MATERIALS

1. Black eyebrow pencil
2. Kleenex tissue

APPLICATION

1.
Dry your teeth with the Kleenex.

2–4.
Keep your mouth open and go over your teeth with the tip of your eyebrow pencil to create a missing or chipped tooth.

You might be required to repeat this process several times during the performance. If so, try experimenting with black masking tape over a dry tooth. You might also try black tooth enamel in liquid form. Brush a few layers over a dry tooth and allow the enamel to dry. To clean it off, rub with a towel. There are also Tooth Black-out, Tooth Red-out, and Tooth Brown-out by Bob Kelly. These are wax in stick form. Apply over a dry tooth and, to remove, rub off with a towel. For "whiter than white" teeth, use white tooth enamel.

1

2

3

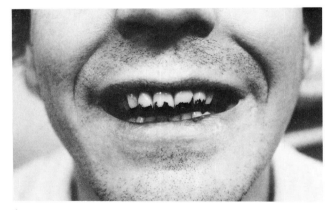

4

Acne

Acne is an inflammatory disease of the oil glands characterized by pimples, which are usually reddish-looking and, in most cases, raised with white heads.

MATERIALS

1. Red lining color (light and dark)
2. Two ⅛″ brushes
3. Black makeup pencil
4. White lining color

APPLICATION

1.

You can create acne by using different tones of red, with a touch of white in the center. This is very time-consuming indeed. Apply the red dots with a brush, then a touch of white in the center, and then go under the white with a sharp, black makeup pencil to create the idea of shadow. This will make the white stand out three-dimensionally, as in the picture.

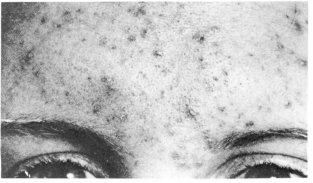

1

Diseased Hand or Face

You can try gelatin and cotton, as explained in Chapter 23 on scars, or the following method.

MATERIALS

1. Liquid latex
2. Bread crumbs
3. Translucent powder and puff
4. Red, brown, or purple lining color

APPLICATION

1.
Apply liquid latex on the area.

2.
Press the bread crumbs into it and wait a few minutes for it to dry.

3.
Cover the entire area with another layer of liquid latex.

4.
Dry, powder, and color it red, brown, or purple.

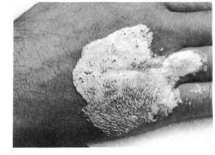

1

2

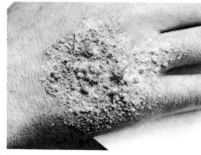

3

4

5

6

5.
Closeup of diseased area.

6.
This may be peeled, stored, and reapplied for future use.

1

2

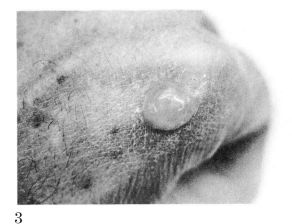

3

Blisters

MATERIALS

1. Kryolan's Tuplast
2. Translucent powder and puff

APPLICATION

1.
Squeeze a small amount of Tuplast over the area and wait until it hardens.

2–3.
Powder gently. It will look like a real blister.

Before using this material, however, test it on a very small area to see how your skin reacts. If the skin reddens and becomes uncomfortable, don't use it.

For broken blisters, use the peeling skin (sunburn) technique.

Burns

MATERIALS

1. Fleshtone color
2. Stipple sponge
3. Liquid latex
4. Kleenex tissue

APPLICATION

1.
Minor burns can be created by stippling the area with a fleshtone color. Depending on the color of your skin, you can make this a lighter or darker shade of fleshtone.

2.
Blisters appear, in most cases, as the result of a burn. To create a blister, check the above explanation. If the blister is a broken one, try the technique used for sunburn and peeling skin.

3–5.
If hanging pieces of skin are desired, use liquid latex on the area: dry, powder, color, gently peel a section of it, and then let it hang. For heavier and longer lasting "hanging skin," use liquid latex, but place a piece of Kleenex tissue on top of it, saturate it again with liquid latex, dry, powder, color, peel a section of it, and let it hang.

6.
Saturate the hanging piece with blood using an eyedropper or a syringe without the needle.

7.
The end result.

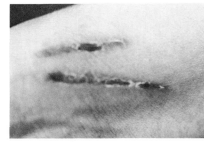

1

2

3

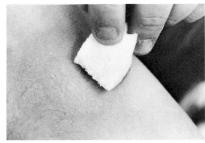

4

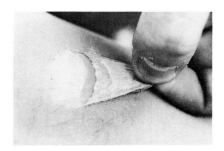

5

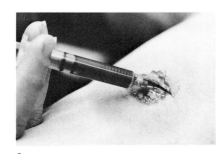

6

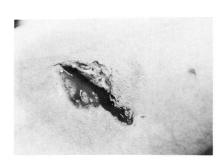

7

Blind Eye with Latex

For the theatre you can create a blind eye with wax or a latex piece; in television and film, use foam latex. You will need someone to help you.

MATERIALS

1. Latex blind eye piece
2. Liquid latex or Duo surgical adhesive
3. Small piece of flesh-colored silk or nylon
4. Foam rubber sponge
5. Hand hair dryer
6. Translucent powder and puff
7. Rubber mask grease
8. Highlight and shadow
9. Off-white or black

APPLICATION

1.
This is a blind eye made of latex.

2.
Before attaching the latex piece, the eyelid must be anchored by applying a touch of liquid latex or Duo surgical adhesive on the upper and lower lids (stay away from the eyelashes).

3.
Cut a piece of flesh-colored silk or nylon, place it over the liquid latex, and let it dry. This will keep your eye closed and alleviate strain from the other eye.

4.
Place a touch of liquid latex at the inner corner of the eye.

5.
Adhere the latex piece to it.

6.
Keep the latex piece out of the way and apply liquid latex gradually to the upper and lower areas of the eye.

1

2

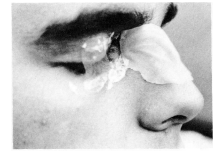

3

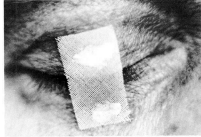

4

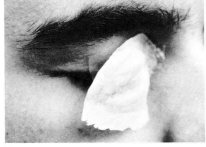

5

6

7.
Place the latex piece, making sure all of its edges are glued and blended to the skin.

8.
Gently go over the entire piece with liquid latex, using a foam rubber sponge as an applicator. Dry with a hand hair dryer and powder.

9.
Color with a shade of rubber mask grease that matches your foundation. Add highlight and shadow, and a touch of off-white or black in the center of the eyepiece.

10.
The final result.

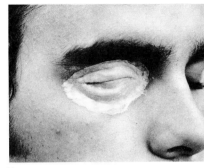

7

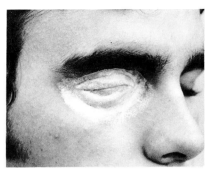

8

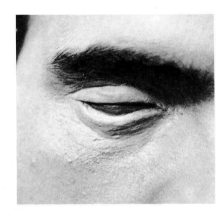

9

10

Blind Eye
with Wax

If you're planning to use wax instead of a latex piece you will need:

MATERIALS

1. Small piece of silk or nylon
2. Wax
3. Liquid latex or Duo surgical adhesive
4. Modeling tools
5. Cold cream
6. Sealer
7. ⅜″ brush
8. Acetone
9. Stipple sponge
10. Rubber mask grease
11. Red-A Creme Stick

APPLICATION

1.

Cover your entire eye area—not just a small section in the center—with a piece of silk or nylon, adhering it with liquid latex or Duo surgical adhesive. Or, if necessary, make the silk piece large enough to cover your eyebrow as well.

2–3.

Place the wax on top and, with your fingers or modeling tools, shape it into the blind eye shape desired. When satisfied, smooth it out with a touch of cold cream, apply a coat of sealer over the wax, and wait until dry. (While waiting, rinse your brush in acetone.) Then texture the eye with a stipple sponge and color it with rubber mask grease—adding, perhaps, a touch of Red-A Creme Stick so it matches

1

2

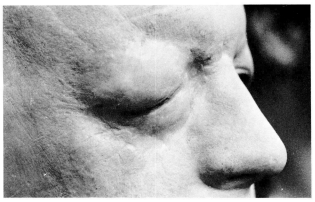

3

the rest of your foundation. For further explanation on wax work, read Chapter 22, Nose and Chin.

All the techniques and ideas suggested here can be used in film and television as well as the theatre. Extreme care must be used in the construction and application of each so it looks as natural and as much a part of the actor's face, hands, and body as possible.

Sources and Materials

BRANDS

What brand of makeup to use? Kelly's, Stein's, Nye's, and others carry the same shades under different names and numbers, and all carry basic tools and materials. The only difference is in the packaging, consistency, and price. Each makeup artist has his own preference depending upon his particular needs. I happen to like Kelly's and Stein's. Leichner, Max Factor and Kryolan are widely used in Great Britain.

Generally speaking, there are three types of makeup base: liquid, pancake, and grease or cream base. Some actresses prefer liquid makeup because they are allergic to other types of foundations. Liquid base, however, is good only for straight makeup.

Actors, actresses, and newscasters on the run often prefer pancake; all makeup companies manufacture it. It is good for straight makeup, but generally has a matte finish with much less life or sheen to it than other bases. Pancake is good for someone with oily skin, since this condition supplies its own sheen. When a lot of people must be ready in a very short time, pancake can be a great timesaver, providing no charac-

ter makeup is involved. Cake makeup comes in all shades; it is applied with a damp sponge and does not require any powder afterwards (used only for straight makeup)—except for Bob Kelly's Rain Barrel, a new concept in cake makeup. This product comes in a wide range of colors, and can be applied with either a damp or dry sponge, or with your fingers. Colors can be blended together as in Creme Stick. It can be used for character makeup, or for highlight and shadow (using wet or dry makeup brushes). When you are finished applying it, furthermore, it is not flat-looking but has a natural sheen that makes it different from all other cake makeups. And, best of all, you can simply wash it off with soap and water.

The most widely used type of makeup for stage, film, and television is cream based. Each company gives it a different name. Kelly calls it "Creme Stick"; Stein calls it "Velvet Stick"; and Factor's is known as "Pan Stick." The cream base makeup comes in all shades and is applied with a dry foam rubber sponge, which gives a thin and smooth coverage. Use your fingers or a natural sponge when you find you need a thicker

coverage.

The list of materials used to create the makeups in this book should give you an idea of what you need in a makeup kit. It is far too cumbersome to carry a kit with all the colors, materials, and tools required for all types of characters. Theatrical cosmetic companies have chosen certain basic colors for their kits. You must learn to mix these few colors in order to get the particular shade you need; and as you add new characters to your repertoire, you will be adding new colors and materials to your makeup kit.

MAKEUP KITS

Any reputable stockist will assemble a general purpose makeup kit for you, which will contain the most obvious and useful materials, according to the price range you have in mind. A visit or letter to the stockist is advisable.

Never—under any circumstances—lend or borrow makeup from anybody, no matter how well you know and trust them. Diseases and infections will not stand up with flags and announce themselves.

SOURCES

Makeup

Costume Unlimited Inc.
184 S. Hotel St. #313
Honolulu, Hawaii 96813

Dooley's Fun Fancy Shoppe
34CO Arctic Blvd.
Anchorage, Alaska 99503

J. J. Products
1441 Kaplocani #1117
Honolulu, Hawaii 96814

Bob Kelly Cosmetics and
Bob Kelly Wig Creation
*Main Office
151 West 46th Street
New York, New York 10036
212-819-0030
*Call or write the main office for
the Bob Kelly makeup distributor nearest you.

Leichner Cosmetics Ltd
599 11th Avenue
New York, New York 10036
212-246-5543

Mikan Theatricals
54 Tide Mill Road
Hampton, New Hampshire
03842
603-926-2744

Mehron, Inc.
250 West 40th Street
New York, New York 10018
212-997-1011

Ben Nye, Inc.
11571 Santa Monica Boulevard
Los Angeles, California 90025
213-478-1558

Ray's Beauty Supply
721 Eighth Avenue
New York, New York 10036
212-757-0175

Paramount Theatrical Supplies
(Alcone)
575 Eighth Avenue
New York, New York
212-594-3980

The Research Council of
Makeup Artists, Inc.
52 New Spaulding Street
Lowell, Massachusetts 01851
617-459-9864

M. Stein Cosmetics Co.
430 Broome Street
New York, New York 10013
212-266-6430

Act I Theatrical Supplies
830 Burrard Street
Vancouver, British Columbia
Canada

Boutique Du Danseur
458 Lindsay
Drummondville, Quebec
Canada

Johnny Brown, Inc.
2019 Mansfield Street
Montreal, Quebec
Canada

Classique Formal & Costume
Rental Ltd.
Penny Lane 513 8th S.W.
Calgary, Alberta
Canada

John Cox
133-10th Avenue, N.E.
Calgary, Alberta T2E 0Y8
Canada

Dance Boutique
1568 Merivale Road
Ottawa, Ontario
Canada

Don's Hobby Shop Co. Ltd.
610-1st Street S.W.
Calgary, Alberta
Canada

Leichner Cosmetics, Inc.
962 W. Broadway
Vancouver, British Columbia
Canada   604-738-3613

Malabar Limited
375 Hargrave Street
Winnipeg, Manitoba
Canada

McCulloch Costume
1034 Dundas Street
London, Ontario
Canada

Pacific Theatrical Supplies Ltd.
P. O. Box 2464
Vancouver, British Columbia
Canada

Joseph Ponton Inc.
451 AT Sulpice Street
Montreal, Quebec
Canada

Shirley Potter Costume
10173-104 Street
Edmonton, Alberta
Canada

Smith of Gainsborough
Attifer Works
Gainsborough, Lincolnshire
England 0427-616 831

The Theatre Zoo Ltd
21 Earlham St
London WC2H 9LL
071-836 3150

Charles H. Fox Ltd
22 Tavistock St
London WC2E 7PY

Kryolan GmbH
Paperstrasse 10
D 1000 Berlin 51

Leichner (London) Ltd
Hawthorne Road
Eastbourne, E. Sussex BN23
6QX

L. Leichner Gmbh
1000 Berlin 37 (Zehlendorf)
Busseallee 13
West Berlin   030-801303132

Fine Music Australia
294 Little Collis Street
Melbourne, Australia

Sweidas Party Ltd.
Queen Street
Brisbane, Queensland
Australia

Headlines
1st Floor Coastland
41 W. Street
Durban 4001
Natal, South Africa   378-137

Nippon Stein Co.
Sunheim Meguro #203, 13-22
Mita 2-Chome, Meguro-Ku
Tokyo, Japan

Oriental Trading Co. Ltd.
Hua Husia Bldg.
14th Floor
64-66 Gloucester Road
Hong Kong

GLOSSARY

Most of the materials and suppliers mentioned throughout this book are American, but some are available in the UK. All of the products listed will have either an alternative or a substitute marketed by the suppliers best known in the UK, ie, Leichner, Max Factor and Kryolan. Any good stockist will be able to advise you here.*

Acetone: This clear liquid is harsh for the skin. It is used to dissolve collodion (scar material) and sealer. Available at drugstores.

Alcohol: Isopropyl alcohol (99% strength) is used to dissolve spirit gum and clean brushes and gummed laces on ready-made beards, mustaches, and wigs. It can be obtained at drugstores.

Artificial Eyelashes: Available at any drugstore or cosmetic counter.

Bald Cap: Theatrical bald cap is available at Mikan Theatricals and Paramount. Bald cap for television and film is available at Kelly's, Leichner's, and also at John Chambers Studio (330 South Myers St., Burbank, Ca. 91506).

Beard: Ready-made beards and mustaches must be ordered ahead of time from Bob Kelly Wig Creation.* In Chapters 15 to 18 the application of beards with crepe hair and crepe wool is discussed in detail.

Beard Block: A wooden block in the shape of a face, used for laying on beards with latex (see Chapter 18), available at wigmakers' supply houses. If not available, a plaster cast of the actor's face can be used (see Chapter 22).

Beard Stubble Black: This waxy material comes in a flat ¼-ounce container, used for one to two days' beard growth. Apply it with a stipple sponge. Available at Kelly's (see Chapter 14).

Bread crumbs: Used to make a diseased hand or face (see Chapter 28).

Blood: For external use, artificial blood is available at Kelly's, Stein's, Nye's, Leichner's, and Paramount. Some companies carry special blood for internal use as well (see Chapter 28).

Blood Capsules: To be filled with cherry or chocolate syrup for internal bleeding. Capsules available at drugstores. A specially-filled blood capsule with a powdered foaming agent for internal use is available at Leichner's (see Chapter 28).

Bobby Pins: See Chapters 20 and 27.

Brushes: Eyebrow brush, rouge brush, lipstick and powder brush, toothbrush; brushes for spirit gum, sealer, collodion, highlight, and shadow. All of these are available at local art stores, Kelly's, Stein's, Nye's, Leichner's, and Paramount.

Cake Eyeliner: Black and brown cake eyeliners are the best to use and should be applied with an eyeliner brush moistened with water. Available at Kelly's, Stein's, Nye's, Leichner's, and Paramount.

Chinese Eyelids: Made of latex, used for creating oriental eyes. Available at Mikan Theatricals (see Chapter 24).

Clay (Roma Plastilina): Clay is the basic material for modeling; it comes in white, gray-green, or yellow-green; soft #1, medium #2, medium firm #3, and very hard #4. Available at art stores and sculpture houses (see Chapter 22).

Cold Cream: For removing makeup and smoothing out wax work. Available at Stein's, Leichner's, and Paramount. Kelly, Stein, and Nye have liquid makeup removers that work well in removing makeup and spirit gum.

Comb: Available locally.

Cotton: Johnson and Johnson's absorbent cotton is invaluable in any makeup kit. Here it is used to create scars (see Chapter 23).

Cream Rouge: Used only over a cream base. Available at Kelly's, Stein's, Nye's, Leichner's, and Paramount.

Creepy Skin: A mixture of soft wax and cotton, available at Illusion House Magical and Theatrical Studios (2617 Herr St., Harrisburg, Pa. 17103).

Crepe Hair: There is a difference between crepe hair and crepe wool. Crepe wool is the familiar

*Theatre Zoo, Charles H. Fox and others provide this service in UK

braided wool we've come to recognize as crepe hair. Crepe hair originally comes straight, like human or yack hair, and is then passed through a special machine to make it "crepey." Currently, crepe wool is hard to find; crepe hair can be used in its place. Both are available at Kelly's, Leichner's, and Paramount (see Chapters 15, 16, and 21).

Curling Iron: These irons are used to curl hair, beards, and mustaches; they come in different thicknesses—the thinnest for mustaches, the thickest for beards and wigs. These have to be heated in an electric stove (see Chapters 18 and 19). Available at Leichner's and Ray's.

Duco Cement: Available at any hardware store. Here it is used in the construction of lifts (see Chapter 27).

Duo Surgical Adhesive: By Mitchum-Thayer, Inc., Tuckahoe, N.Y. 10707, it is used instead of liquid latex for the application of eyelashes.

Eyebags: Different sizes of these latex pieces are available at Kelly's. They are used for aging (see Chapter 12).

Eyebrow Pencils: Available in black, light, medium, and dark brown at all makeup manufacturers and local cosmetic counters.

Eyedropper: A plastic eyedropper is used for dropping tear materials into the eyes. Available at drugstores (see Chapter 28).

Eyeshadows: Eyeshadows come in a variety of shades. Obtainable at Kelly's, Stein's, Nye's,

Paramount, and Leichner's.

Foundations: Basic foundations (one or a combination of many) used in this book are: For Caucasians, male or female: Golden Tan, Natural Tan, 725FN, Suntone, Olive, Lady Fair, CV4W, CV5W; For black performers, male and female: Light and dark Negro, Light and Dark Egyptian, BK1, BK2, SC51 to SC54. CVIW, Pink C2, and White are used as highlight. 32E and Violet SL17 lining color are used as shading.

725N Creme Stick: I have mixed this with other colors to get the right shade for all my models. I have also substituted 725FN for male and female rouge and for general healthy looking skin tone. Red, Yellow, and Green Creme Sticks have been used here and there for a more natural look. All of these Creme Sticks are available at Kelly's, and Paramount. Comparable shades are available at Stein's, Nye's, and Leichner's.

Female Rouge: Female rouge comes in cream or cake and is available at Kelly's, Stein's, Nye's, and Paramount. Cream rouge is used over cream base, and cake rouge over cake makeup, or after the face is powdered.

Fall: A period hair piece is used only if you have long hair to match its length. Available at Kelly's (see Chapter 20).

Flesh-colored Silk or Nylon: A small amount of this is used to construct lifts, or to anchor the eyelid down for creating a blind eye (see Chapters 27 and 28).

Foam Rubber Sponge: Available at Kelly's, Stein's, and at de-

partment stores. Used for application of basic foundation (see Chapters 2, 3, 4, etc.).

Glycerin: At Bob Kelly it is called "Tears and Perspiration." You can also get it at your local drugstore (see Chapter 28).

Hair Dryer: Available locally.

Hair Spray: Available locally.

Hair Whitener: Available in liquid form, in white, off-white, and yellow. In stick form it comes in off-white, yellow, and blue-gray (M22B), all obtainable at Kelly's, Stein's, Nye's, Leichner's, and Paramount (see Chapters 1, 9, and 10).

Hand Mirror with a magnifying side, available locally.

Heavy Duty Thread: In black, brown, or white, it is used in the construction of lifts (see Chapter 27).

Hooks and Eyes: Discard the "eyes" and keep the "hooks" for the construction of lifts (see Chapter 27).

Japanese Brush: Available at any art store in different sizes. Used to paint liquid latex inside molds; also used to paint bald caps, noses, or scars.

Kleenex: In addition to its general use, here it is used for aging combined with liquid latex (see Chapter 11).

Knox Gelatin: The gelatin is used by itself or mixed with cotton for scars (see Chapter 28).

Latex Pieces: Mikan Theatricals carries a variety of ready made latex scars, moles, bruises, wounds, chins, noses, eyebags, wrinkled foreheads, blind eyes, etc.

Lipsticks: Kelly's, Stein's, Nye's, Leichner's, and Paramount carry a variety of shades for your kit.

Liquid Latex: Used to make small latex pieces; used alone on the face to create aging (see Chapter 10); and, when combined with Kleenex, to create extreme old age (see Chapter 11). Available at Kelly's, Stein's, and Paramount.

Makeup Remover: See *Cold Cream*.

Male Lipcolor: Available at Kelly's and Leichner's; or, you can mix a little gray and red with a touch of fleshtone for the right shade.

Male Rouge: Used to warm up a face, to give it a youthful or healthy look. Available at Kelly's, Stein's, Nye's, Leichner's, and Paramount.

Mascara: Cake, roll-on, or liquid mascara in black or brown is available at Kelly's, Stein's, Nye's, Leichner's, and Paramount, or at the local cosmetic counter.

Mustache: A lace mustache can be ordered from Kelly's; or, you can lay one on with crepe or natural hair (see Chapters 16, 17, and 19).

Mutton Chops: These can be made on latex or laid on with crepe hair or synthetic fibers; or, they can be ordered from Kelly's (see Chapter 19).

Orange Wood Stick: Used to press down artificial eyelashes, to create a cut in a wax scar, or as a modeling tool. Available at drugstores (see Chapter 22).

Plaster of Paris: Used to make positive or negative molds.

Available at hardware stores (see Chapter 22).

Plastic Adhesive: Used instead of spirit gum for prosthetic pieces and bald caps in film and television. Available at Kelly's.

Plastic Sheet or Saran Wrap: Used to take the measurement or pattern of the head or face. (For ordering the right size wig or beard, see Chapters 17–21.)

Powder, Translucent: This particular powder does not change the color of makeup. Available at Kelly's, Stein's, Nye's, Leichner's, and Paramount.

Powder Puff: A few clean puffs are necessary in any makeup kit.

Q-Tips: Keep a box in your makeup kit.

Razor Blade, Single-Edged: A necessary item in any makeup kit. Used instead of scissors for cutting lace beards, etc.—and, of course, for sharpening pencils (see Chapter 22).

Red-A Creme Stick: This particular shade of Creme Stick can be stippled over latex or wax pieces to give them a natural texture and look. Available at Kelly's (see Chapters 22–25).

Red Rubber Sponge: This sponge is used as an applicator for Red-A Creme Stick or Beard Stubble Black. Available at Kelly's and Woolworth's.

Roux Hair Crayon: This crayon, available in black and brown, comes in a lipstick shade and is used to darken gray hairs. Available at drugstores and at Paramount. Applied with a wet toothbrush or eyebrow brush (see Chapter 1).

Rubber Bands: These have many uses. Two of the very small sizes are used in the construction of lifts (see Chapter 27).

Rubber Mask Grease: Makeup with a special castor-oil base, especially formulated for use over latex or foam rubber prosthetic pieces. Available in six shades from Kelly's and Paramount. To make it, mix a small amount of castor oil with powdered pancake, mix well to the proper consistency, add a few drops of acetone, and leave it with the top open for the acetone to evaporate.

Sealer: Sealer is a clear liquid, obtainable from Kelly's, Nye's, Leichner's, and Paramount. Used as a protection over wax or clay noses and chins, it dissolves in acetone (see Chapters 22–26).

Scar Material: This non-flexible collodion is used to simulate deep cuts in the skin for scars. It should not be used on children, near the eyes, or on very sensitive skins. Available at Kelly's, Stein's, Nye's, Leichner's, and Paramount (see Chapter 23).

Scotch Tape: This particular tape can be used to create droopy eyelids or oriental eyes. Available at Woolworth's and stationery stores (see Chapter 28).

Scissors: The most important tool in a makeup kit.

Sideburns: You can grow them for the part, if you have time, or order them from Kelly's. You can also lay them on using crepe hair, or natural or synthetic fibers (see Chapter 19).

Silk Cloth: Because silk is lint free, it is ideal for pressing lace pieces over spirit gum (see Chapter 16).

Saran Wrap: See *Plastic Sheet.*

Spatula: For mixing colors, for application and blending of wax pieces. A general and valuable tool for any makeup kit (see Chapters 22–23).

Stipple Sponge: This small black sponge should be pressed gently over wax or clay to give it texture. Available at Kelly's, Stein's, and Paramount (see Chapters 22–25).

Spirit Gum: A liquid adhesive used to glue beards, mustaches, wigs, and bald caps. Regular spirit gum has a certain shine and is used in the theatre. For television and film, matte spirit gum is preferred. It is advisable to leave the cap off the jar ahead of time to get it thick and gummy. Available at Kelly's, Stein's, Nye's, Paramount, and Leichner's.

Stage Lining Colors: Lining colors are available at Kelly's, Stein's, Nye's, Paramount, and Leichner's.

Stubble Beard Adhesive: A clear wax in a tube, available at Kelly's. It is rubbed over the skin or over the bald cap before adding chopped hairs (see Chapters 14–25).

Soap: Besides its obvious use,

it is used for lubricating the brushes used in making latex pieces.

Syrup: Chocolate or cherry syrup is used inside the clear capsule (see *Blood Capsule*). For internal use.

Thinning Shears: This special scissors is used to thin thick hairs, beards, or wigs. Available at hair supply houses (see Chapter 21).

Tooth Black-out, Tooth Red-out, Tooth Brown-out: These are wax in stick form for use over a dry tooth. Available at Kelly's (see Chapter 28).

Toothbrush: A wooden, unpainted toothbrush is ideal for cleaning hairpieces, if you are using acetone; if you are using alcohol, a regular toothbrush will do. Either brush can be used for hair touchups.

Tooth Enamel: This is a liquid, and comes in black and white. Brush a few layers over a dry tooth and allow to dry. Remove by rubbing off with a towel. Available at Leichner's, Stein's, and Paramount (see Chapter 28).

Toothpick: For pressing down artificial eyelashes or making a cut in a wax piece.

Translucent Powder: See *Powder.*

Tuplast: This is a liquid plastic in a tube, which is used to create scars or blisters. If you have very sensitive skin, stay away from this material. Available at Paramount (see Chapter 28).

Tweezers: A handy tool for attaching eyelashes, applied either in strips or individually; for lifting corners of the latex pieces; and, of course, for plucking eyebrows. Available at all drugstores (see Chapter 12).

Vaseline: Prevents casting materials or plaster from sticking to hair, eyebrows, and eyelashes. A good item to have in a makeup kit (see Chapter 22).

Wax: Used to build up a new nose or chin, cover eyebrows, or create scars. For the best results, use a coat of spirit gum under the wax. Available at Kelly's, Stein's, Paramount, Nye's, and Leichner's (see Chapters 22–26).

If you are using one brand of makeup exclusively you can order it directly from the manufacturer or distributor in your area (write for a brochure). If you have a makeup kit with mixed colors and material from different companies, it is advisable to order your materials from a makeup supply house that carries all brands.

LEE BAYGAN

Lee Baygan has been director of makeup for the National Broadcasting Company (NBC) since 1966 and has been twice nominated for an Emmy for his work in daytime television drama and in an NBC special. Originally educated in both music and drama, he continued his studies in New York and is a graduate of the American Academy of Dramatic Arts and the City College of New York, where he studied film technique and production. A lecturer in the art of makeup, Lee has taught at the Yale School of Music and the Yale School of Drama, currently teaches at C.W. Post Center, Long Island University, and conducts special lectures and workshops in makeup for regional theatres, community theatres, colleges and universities, theatre festivals, and conventions across the country. His first two books, one on the theatre, *Behind the Velvet Curtain*, and one on television, *On the Blue Sky*, were published abroad. He has also written *Techniques of Three-Dimensional Makeup*, which deals with prosthetics, a highly specialized and technically complex area of makeup. Lee continues his interest in music, and he composes for classical guitar and for flute and guitar.